DEEP

DEEP

ALIVE WITH PURPOSE
ROB MURPHY

Open Gates Entertainment & Sports - DEEP, The Life of Rob Murphy may be purchased for educational, business or sales promotional use.

First Edition - Volume 1

Photographs by - Rick Osentoski, Steve King & Dennis Nett
Eastern Michigan Media Relation Office, Syracuse Post Standard

Edits by - Victoria Sun, Janette Ellis & Nikki Borges

Dear RJ & Ryann,

I am not perfect. I have achieved some amazing things, and I have made many mistakes. I have really good days, and sometimes I have awful ones. I don't know everything, and I won't always have the right answer because like you, I'm still learning and growing, too. And despite all of this, I am still your superhero. The two of you have enriched my life in so many ways, and I am so incredibly thankful.

Know that every story after this page will always lead me back to you. You are what I'm most proud of. If you're ever lost, look back to this page and be reminded that my love for you exceeds the perimeter of the whole universe. You are more important to me than anything in the world, and I am ALWAYS here for you, through the ups and downs, near or far, no matter how bad the subject may seem. Find comfort in the fact that you can share ANYTHING with me; trust me, I will understand. I am proud of all you both have accomplished so far, and I'm even prouder of all I know you will achieve in the future.

RJ - Arge in charge!

Bud, you are extremely special. As you navigate life, hold onto what makes you different. It will be your difference that will make you a star at whatever it is you do in your life. Never lose your wonderful imagination, others may miss your message because they can't see the magic unfolding in your head. It is your sensitivity and brilliance that make you more aware than others around you, not only of things that are good, but also the things that aren't quite right in the world. Be a beacon of light and hope for us all. If you can do that, you will change the world. And don't forget that even when I'm not with you, I am standing right behind you and backing you up. ALWAYS!

Ryann - My booper dooper super trooper ☺

You are unstoppable and don't forget it. Let that bold sense humor and confidence lead you; believe in yourself! You have everything you need right inside of you to be anything you want to be. Don't change, just evolve into the powerful strong woman you are destined to become. Keep following your instincts and trust your gut, 97% of the time, it will be right. You can't see it right now, but one day you will learn that you are way ahead of the game when it comes to understanding life. Stay tough for me! Keep smiling and keep shining baby girl!

I love you guys with every molecule in my heart. No matter where I am, I'm thinking of you and smiling.

Love,

Dad

CONTENTS

INTRODUCTION

After years of contemplation and hesitation, I've mustered enough courage to share my story. During this process, I embraced being vulnerable in order to share my truth. My life exemplifies the statement, "What doesn't kill you makes you stronger." I'm living proof that all you overcome can push you to be the best version of yourself. It is important to understand that others are always watching, listening and depending on you, so you must act, speak and think about how your actions, words and leadership affects others. Every struggle, every bit of pain, and each hardship I experienced was actually a gift from God. These hardships allowed me to remain focused on my own development while being a mentor and leader to others. The essential nature of being alive is to experience life in its purest form…the wins and losses, the celebrations and challenges, and the good with the bad. Remember, through darkness comes light, through fear comes love, and through struggle comes success.

Throughout life, we will all have someone or something we turn to during our darkest moments. It is important that who or what you turn to helps you stay on the right track and gives you a sense of comfort and strength. During my darkest times, I always turned to music of all genres, which I still do today. Hip Hop music took over my sole at a very young age.

I enjoyed several rappers throughout my childhood, but the day I heard Shawn Carter, aka, Jay Z in 1996, he became my favorite. While everyone was arguing about who was the best MC between Tupac and Biggie Smalls, I always said Jay Z was better than them both (long before he became a household name).

I remember listening to *I Love the Dough on* Biggie's album, *Life After Death*, which featured Jay Z and Angela Winbush on the hook, sampled over her hit song *I Love You More,* which was released in 1981. Angela's song brought back memories of my mother, as she used to play it when I was a child. To hear it paried with Biggie and Jay Z rapping over it, was amazing. A month later, Jay Z's *In My Lifetime* album was released and he became the main rap artist I would listen to for the next 20 years. Song by song, I felt some form of connection to his stories. As I eagerly waited for the next album, I felt we were growing together year by year. Listening to his music was a way for me to express myself and relate. His lyrics empowered me to keep moving forward. The movie *Streets is Watching* and the documentary *Fade to Black,* are works of art I watched over and over for entertainment. Detroit, New York City, Miami and Los Angeles are all places I watched him in concert, and every time, his performance was EPIC. I always felt as if it was my first time watching him perform.

Sixteen albums and twenty two years later, the majority of my playlist still consists of Jay Z. There are several great artists which I've given a listening opportunity, but no one has come close to having the same effect as Jay Z. Starting with *Can't Knock the Hustle* (*Reasonable Doubt* - Album) to *Love Happy* (*The Carters*) it's been a pleasurable ride. There's been lots education, growth, partying and relaxing to his music for over two decades. With every album, remix, and collaboration, I continue to appreciate Jay Z, the storyteller. Now, I'm compelled to share my story too, because in some way, shape or form, I believe that my journey will inspire your own.

Chapter One

LUCKY ME

There's this incredible energy in the air, as fans begin to pour into the arena. A distinct smell of popcorn, pizza, and nachos with jalapeños immediately hits your nose as the lines begin to form at the entry. Glancing back and forth at their ticket stubs, everyone is eager to find their section. DJ Khaled's *All I Do is Win*, featuring T-Pain, Ludacris, Snoop Dogg, and Rick Ross, is booming in the background. T-Pain's demand for everyone to put their hands up when the hook drops puts a rhythm in your step. Excitement is continuing to build. Below, we see the players finishing up their last round of warm ups and getting in the zone.

In the blink of an eye, the entire arena has filled with 8,919 fans and is submerged in green and white. Suddenly, it's time. All at once, a collaborative pulse propels us to our feet, and the crowd projects a rioting, "Let's go Eagles!" clap-clap, clap-clap-clap. The lights suddenly cut to black, and from the Jumbotron, the game opening video demands all eyes. "Ladies and gentlemen, please welcome your 2019/2020 Men's Basketball team!" The crowd unleashes a thunderous roar as the greatest arena rock song of all time, *We*

Will Rock You by Queen, rushes over the speakers. The start of the college basketball season has officially begun.

After the line-ups are announced, it's time to take the stage. But first, the team heads to a huddle for one final word, and they all look to me. Standing there in the daze, I snap out of it. I am on the court completely surrounded by the eyes of sixteen eager players, all waiting on my queue.

"Coach! Whatchá got for us?"

I quickly clear my throat, "It's the first game of the season, and this is OUR home court! You know what to do! Let's go! Defense on 3! 1, 2, 3!" I take my seat on the bench in an arena engulfed with green and white, and I pinch myself. Is this really happening? How in the world did I get here?

I grew up in a single-parent household in one of the roughest Detroit neighborhoods in the 1970s. We lived on the west side of town, typically referred to as Dexter & Linwood. Thugs, drug dealers, and gang bangers shared the streets with the vagrants, crackheads, and regular working-class folks just trying to make it. It didn't take long for me to get used to the sound of gunshots and the sight of illegal activities at an early age. Dexter & Linwood was one of the many low-income, poverty-stricken areas that made up the inner city of Detroit. But to me, it was just home, a place I loved.

Throughout my life, I only met my father twice, and quite frankly, I barely remember those two visits, let alone his name. It was clear that he had absolutely no desire to know me, which frustrated my mom most. I, on the other hand, felt indifferent about the situation. It was my mother's frustration that upset me rather than the fact that I was abandoned by my own father. After all, how can you miss something you never had in the first place?

My mom and I lived on the top floor of a duplex on Calvert Street with my grandmother, Annie Mae and my favorite Uncle Skeeter. They all called me Chick because my skin had a bright yellow undertone that was, to them, similar to a baby chicken. I had the lightest skin complexion in my entire family. Uncle Skeeter stood 6'5" with a huge afro. He would throw me on his shoulders and take me all around the neighborhood, morning to night. Folks would routinely shoot dice on the corner, and children would run around the playground and play pick-up on the basketball court nearby.

I felt invincible with Uncle Skeeter. At the time, he was the only man I had in my life to look up to, so naturally, we grew extremely close. It wasn't until I turned five that I really began to understand that my biological father was nonexistent in my life.

My mother, Andrea Jean Murphy, gave birth to me when she was sixteen years old, and I am the spitting image of her. She had a smooth caramel complexion, and a petite delicate frame. Her almond brown eyes sat behind stylish glasses, and she dressed in the trendiest outfits from head to toe. Her beauty was amplified when her face broke into a smile. That smile of hers was brighter than a crescent moon in the night sky. When I look in the mirror, I see her face every time. The first impression she gave was sweet and docile. But beneath those qualities was an outspoken and strong young woman with unwavering confidence.

She was truly a phenomenal human being. All of her friends characterized her as a giver, a person who would do anything for anyone. She's the kind of person who would set aside all personal needs just to make everyone else happy. The kind of person you'd be lucky to come by, selfless. To this day, I have never met another person who has been as generous as her; it's from her that I learned to live life the very same way.

For any teenager, raising a child is a challenge. Although my mom was years ahead of her age, it was still difficult. But through it all, she devoted a great deal of time and energy to mold me into a proper young man. I continue to carry on small habits she instilled in me from a young age. She was a stickler for hygiene and organization. I had to brush my teeth after every meal, iron my clothes before bed each night, and make my bed every morning. When it came to teaching me good habits and discipline, my mom did not play.

The summer before I turned six, we moved to Santa Rosa Street, in an area known as the 7 Mile, BK territory. Our house sat snugly in the center of a long block, surrounded by patches of grass and lots of trees. It was a small, square-shaped house with an A-frame roof and chimney. We had a barely paved walkway that led to a grey front door, which sat left of a small window. It was slightly better than the home we had before, but we were still in a poor area of Detroit.

The houses on my block were small and spaced closely together. You could take five steps from one house to the next. Iron bars covered the doors and windows of every house for protection. While the neighborhood had a few boarded-up houses and businesses, most people took pride in the upkeep of their front lawns.

In our new house, Uncle Skeeter lived in the basement. It was during my time in the basement with Uncle Skeeter that my love for music was born. Marvin Gaye, Stephanie Mills, The Jackson 5, Teddy Pendergrass, Aretha Franklin, and The Whispers, are some of the artists that were on constant replay, as well as my all-time favorite song, *Rapper's Delight* by the Sugar Hill Gang. There was a fully loaded refrigerator with all sorts of snacks and juice, and a stocked bar with every liquor you could imagine. If I could have hung out down there all the time, I would have. But on certain days, the basement was completely off limits, and under no circumstances was I allowed to take even one step into the basement…

When I came home from school on any given Friday evening, I would walk into a house full of people. Our house was the spot for all sorts of gatherings, cookouts, birthday parties…you name it! The whole neighborhood was welcome to stop by and enjoy whatever they pleased, and so they did. The music was always bumping, food was always cooking, and we were always having a good time. But under the surface of the fun, like in most hoods, there was gambling, drinking, and lots of drugs. I can still hear my mother shouting at me, "Get outta here, Chick! Promise me you won't ever do none of this stuff you see!" But all of the secrecy only made me more curious.

My inquisitiveness always led me to the basement on those days I wasn't supposed to go down there. What were they trying to hide from me? I desperately needed to see. So, one day when my mom and grandmother were gone, I snuck half way down the steps and quietly peeked over the banister. I saw various groups of men making stacks of aluminum packages filled with drugs. There were scales, heroin, cocaine, tablespoons, sifters, and more cash than I had ever seen, neatly organized on the bar, right when you entered the basement. I wasn't too sure what to make of it, but as I got older, it didn't take long for me to understand what was going on. The pipes, needles, and syringes on the table would eventually have meaning. Our house was a stash house.

When my mom was eighteen, she met a guy who made her undeniably happy. His name was Hosea "Bullet" Payne, but people just called him by his street name, Bullet. Four years later, at twenty-two years old, my mom and Bullet had a baby boy, James Bullet Payne. We called my little brother "Woo" because he had more energy than anyone could handle. And my grandmother would always let out this sigh, "whew," when she was out of breath from chasing him around. He wore her out! I was officially a big brother and excited to no longer be an only child. Bullet moved in with us after he and my mom married. Bullet was the first man I was truly able to call "Dad."

Looking back, my life wasn't as structured as I thought it was. I missed out on the first two years of school and didn't start until I was six. The kids in my class at Hampton Elementary had already learned the basics from preschool to kindergarten, and I was so behind. At that point in my life, I had no concept of what school meant, never opened a single book, nor did I know how to read or write. My grandmother took time to read me bedtime stories, but that was not enough to help my transition to school, so it was a major adjustment for me. I had never been away from my family, let alone left the neighborhood, the entire first five years of my life. Adding to my trauma was the fact that I didn't know how to interact with other children. I had spent all of my time hanging with Uncle Skeeter and adults and barely played with any kids my age.

When I wasn't in school, I started spending time with the neighborhood kids. Kadeja was the girl next door, who I specifically remember constantly bickering with. Back then, I had very little interaction with girls, so it all makes sense to me now. On the opposite side of Kadeja's house lived three sisters, Kenya, Cassandra, and Samantha. I literally lived on a street full of girls! I bet it would surprise you all that I still know how to play hop scotch, rockin' robin, and jump rope. We were all just kids having fun and didn't know any different. But we were children growing up in the midst of one of the nation's roughest neighborhoods, riddled by violence, drugs, and crime. It was 1978, and Detroit was ruled by several drug gangs, most notably Young Boys Incorporated and Pony Down, led by known kingpins Frank Nitty, Raymond Peoples, and Sylvester Murray.

After repeatedly watching what went down when the basement was supposed to be off limits, I had inadvertently become a young expert. I was in fourth grade when I started to replicate cutting heroin and cocaine using baby powder. I would shut my bedroom door and sit on the top bunk pretending to prepare a drug package. I snuck a sifter to dice the baby powder up, and used a playing card to section it off, level it and cut it while it sat on an album cover. At the tender age of nine years old, I had it all down, but didn't understand that I was imitating an illegal activity.

When my grandmother caught me in the act one day, she was so shocked that she nearly had a heart attack. To her relief, it was only baby powder. However, my understanding of what I was mimicking was very concerning to her.

Early one morning in August of 1981, the piercing sound of rapid and repetitive gunshots woke me from my sleep. Although it was a sound I had heard many times before, the blast of the gunshots sent a shock throughout my entire body every single time. I was so frozen by the reverberation that I couldn't move to get up and see what was going on. Moments after the noise faded, the sound of sirens filled the air and I was still unsure of just how close the gunfire was. Once the chaos subsided, my grandmother came to check on me, and told me to go back to sleep.

When I woke up, my mother wasn't home. But she was always on the go, so it wasn't unusual for her not to be there when I got up. My grandmother acted the same as she always did; therefore, I assumed that my mom was just out and about. I ended up not seeing her or Bullet until the following evening when they returned from the hospital. I learned that the gunshots I heard were aimed at them as they were walking into the house. Someone was trying to kill them. One of the bullets grazed the edge of my mother's left eye, causing her to become partially blind. Bullet was also hit, but by the grace of God, they both survived.

I eventually found out that my mother was part of a drug operation. And as time progressed, I learned not only did she sell drugs, but she was one of THE BIGGEST drug dealers in Detroit.

When I discovered that the men in the basement worked for my mother, and that she was the one in charge, I wasn't really shocked by it because I didn't completely understand. I still had no idea exactly what drugs were, let alone that they were illegal to distribute. This was my life and I didn't know any different. When I look back at my childhood, IT BLOWS MY MIND.

My mother was a bonafide hustler who never worked a regular job a single day of her life. With multiple people working for her, she was the drug queen of several neighborhoods. Like my mom, Bullet had a huge role in the drug game. Together, the two of them joined territories and became so powerful that they were a threat to other dealers. Working and living together made my mother and Bullet easy targets for rivals who wanted them dead.

Day-to-day, they were living in a state of fear and paranoia. A year after they were shot, my mother was forced to separate from the love of her life. In the interest of everyone's safety, Bullet made the sacrifice and left us.

When Bullet left, it was earth shattering. The role he filled for both my mother and I was one we once lacked. For me, he was a father figure. Like many father-son dynamics, I sought his approval on just about everything and emulated his behavior because I wanted to be just like him. Before Bullet, I wondered once in a while, what was so wrong with me that my own father wanted nothing to do with my life? Bullet's involvement and support built up my self-esteem. Everything I was missing, I found in him. So, I was really hurt when he left, and at the time, I took it personally. I was yet again left fatherless, and didn't understand why.

For my mother, well, this was devastating for her. Bullet was her everything. He was the love of her life, her best friend, her teammate, her ride or die. In our environment, it was typical to have people in and out of your life, but his departure was a tough one to handle.

As time moved on, the loss of Bullet became easier, and life reverted back to normal. A couple of years later, my mom met a wholesome man named Ray Coleman. By then, she was twenty-four years old. Ray was different from any other guy she ever dealt with because he was the first man she dated who wasn't from the streets or in the drug business. He came from a church-going family, and brought the religious presence of God to our household. Ray was the one who took me to church for the first time. I wasn't as close to Ray as I was with Bullet, but his spiritual impact guided me. At twenty-six years old, it was with Ray that my mother had her third and final child, Ray Coleman Jr.

In our home, my brothers and I never saw the normalcy of what everyday life was actually like for the average person. Because of this, my mother made it a priority for us to spend time with "normal" families, to show us another side of life and ultimately keep us safe from her business.

When I was about nine years old, my mom introduced us to two families that have played vital roles in who I've become. Both the Cottrell and Washington families were two-parent households who demanded discipline and responsibility from their children. Gloria Cottrell was Bullet's sister. She married Robert Cottrell and together they had three children, Brian, Le Le, and Torin. Spending time on Tracey Street with the Cottrells quickly became my favorite place on the weekends. Their house was about ten minutes from mine, and even though it was also in a rough area, it was safer than being home in the midst of my mother's dealings. They were a middle-class family, and Robert and Gloria both worked 9-to-5 jobs to make a living the right way. They made just enough money to pay the bills and provide for their children.

Soon the Cottrells were like family to me and my favorite place to be! Uncle Rob really showed me what it was to be a man and how to live life the correct way. He was a true innovator who started his own job employment agency called Career Works. He exemplified the definition of a leader. Aunt Gloria was a strong working woman who preached the importance of academics. She was very integral in fighting to save the Dodge Main plant, while working at UAW local 7. Brian was the older brother I never had. From him, I learned so many different things, most notably, how to ride a BMX bike. Brian was one of the nation's fastest BMX riders, which inspired Torin and me to fall in love with the sport. Soon I became one of the fastest '10 & under' racers in Michigan.

Torin, who was the same age as me, became my best friend. Watching the *Dukes of Hazzard* on Friday nights, and *Scooby Doo* and *Woody Woodpecker* on Saturday mornings was our thing. Le Le was our big sister. She was a great example academically, and was very supportive and patient with us. I couldn't have been happier spending time with the Cottrells. It felt comforting to be around people living the right way. I was just a kid, but I could feel the difference. Being able to witness a husband and wife work as a team to make an honest living and raise three children had a profound influence on what I wanted for my future.

From the Washington family, I gained a completely different insight that added value to my life. Tyrone and Durinda Washington were two of the kindest people I had ever met. My mother and Tyrone developed a friendship through their work together in the drug business. The Washington's were raising thirteen children in a three-bedroom, one-bathroom ranch style house that was about 1,300 square feet. During the time I spent there, I was forced to share and be thoughtful. Tyrone and Durinda wouldn't have it any other way.

When I stayed with the Washington's, I was pushed to join the Cobras Youth Organization little league football team. Tyrone, Jr. was a few years older than me, and the coolest kid I had ever met. He was the varsity little league star quarterback who had the best shag haircut and a charm that drew in all the cheerleaders. I looked up to him so much, and with his guidance, I became the star running back for the Cobras junior varsity team. My first ever football coach, Greg Cannon, tried to keep me grounded but my athletic ability allowed me to start developing confidence and an ego. After seeing and understanding more than the average child my age, I thought I had it figured out. No one could tell me nothin'.

Ray and my mom were now three years into their relationship, and things weren't working out. I never understood exactly what caused them to break up, but another man who filled the fatherly role was walking out of my life yet again, and this time I was affected by the change a little differently.

En route to Hampton Elementary, I'd stop at a convenience store each morning to buy candy. I used the money my mother gave me for lunch to stock up on as many treats as I could, then sell them to my classmates for more than I paid. At school, my teachers were constantly warning me to put the candy away because students were not allowed to sell anything on the school premises. One day during science class, the teacher prompted me to empty my pockets that were clearly stuffed with Now and Later candy. When I refused to do it, the teacher tried reaching into my pockets herself, so I pushed her. She fell to the ground and the entire class gasped. When I saw my teacher sprawled out across the floor of the classroom, I felt regretful and worried. I was suspended immediately, and brought back for a hearing two weeks later. It was the first major mistake I made in my life. And why, I wonder? I mean, I knew better than to push a teacher. Maybe I was tired of my mom being upset after her break up with Ray, and how it was affecting things at home. Or perhaps I felt rules didn't apply to me because my mom was the boss. Or was it that she was so stressed running a drug operation that she didn't have as much time for me? Could this mistake stem from the fact that I simply needed attention? I couldn't see it then, but looking back, this moment seemed like a cry for help.

The principal eventually decided to expel me for being violent with a teacher. Seeing the expression on my grandmother's face when she heard the news made me realize how badly I messed up. For the next forty days, my mom and grandmother tried everything they could to get me into another school, but no one would accept me. This fueled my grandmother's anger with me even more. I was a complete disappointment to her.

When no one else would accept me, Dr. David Porter at Bagley Elementary stepped in and gave me a chance. That incident curbed my ego, and proved to me that every action comes with a consequence. I spent my fifth and sixth grade years at Bagley with a new attitude, and it turned out to be the ideal place for me to land. For a kid who was once behind, I graduated in pretty good academic standing. I started the seventh grade at Beaubien Middle School, and was spending a lot more time on Tracey Street with the Cottrell family.

On a random Tuesday before my mother dropped me off at the Cottrell's house, she got into a huge argument over the phone. I specifically remember her saying, "He wants to take my men and run my territory!" When I attempted to find out what was going on, she evaded the topic. When we arrived at the Cottrell's house, and my mother and Aunt Gloria sat in the den talking for hours. It was obvious something serious was happening. Eventually, my mother came to say goodbye, and I knew from the way she looked at me, she was worried. Her eyes said it all.

The evening went as it typically did. After finishing our homework, we watched a movie, played video games, and ate Buddy's pizza. It was a blast per usual. However, when it was time for me to be picked up the following evening, my mom asked if I could stay at the Cottrell's one more night. Yes! What child doesn't love an extended sleepover? But the same exact thing happened the following day.

By Thursday, I was ready to go home. When I spoke to my mom that day after school, she said she would pick me up from the Cottrell's house shortly. Finally, I would get to sleep in my own bed! I packed up my belongings and watched television as I waited for her to arrive. One episode of *The Jeffersons* turned into an episode of *Sanford & Son*, then an episode of *Benny Hill* came on, and before I knew it, the black of night had completely rolled in. It was almost midnight, and no one could get in touch with my mother. I ended up spending another night at the Cottrell's.

The following day, November 1, 1985, would be a day that changed my life forever. School was going as it normally did. The hot lunch menu had fish sticks, I hung out with my girlfriend LaDonna Sims at recess, and I even got a "B" on an English test I didn't study for. It was 2:15 p.m. in my last period class when I gazed up at the clock above the chalk board anxiously awaiting the bell to ring. To pass the time, I started doodling on my notebook. Seconds later, the intercom rang through to our classroom.

"Ms. Donahue, can you please send Robert Murphy to the main office?"

My heart dropped as I packed up my stuff. On the way, I bounced ideas back and forth in my head. What could I have possibly done to get called down to the office? To my surprise, it was just Uncle Rob coming to pick me up early. Whew, what a relief! I was a little confused, but happy to leave school early. On the way to the car, I asked why he came to pick me up. But my uncle was extremely tense and kept quiet.

"Did I do something?" I asked. He continued to walk ahead of me to the car, but didn't say anything. By then, I was getting more and more anxious. I threw my backpack in the trunk, sat in the passenger's seat, and looked him right in the eye.

"What did I do?" I shouted. I could tell it was hard for him to look at me.

"Robert, I don't know how to say this to you, but I was sent to be the one to tell you…"

He looked away from me out the opposite window and took a deep breath, followed by a long pause. I sat back quietly and waited for him to compose himself. An overwhelming energy that was smothering him made it clear that this was difficult.

Three breaths and four heart beats later, he cleared his throat and slowly said, "Ummm, last night your mother, ummm, your mother, she was shot… she was shot and killed last night… I'm so sorry."

My face transformed into one of sheer disbelief. "Huh? What?" I stared back into my uncle's eyes and then turned away. Everything around me suddenly stopped. The world became completely silent, and in slow motion my brain processed this. I could hear the sound of my racing heartbeat louder than I've ever heard it before. My breath sped up, my eyes slowly blinked twice, and without control I punched the car window as hard as I could. All at once, tears came pouring down my face. This would be the day that changed my life forever.

Chapter Two

THIS CAN'T
BE LIFE

N o matter how much time passes, it is still impossible for me to
fully articulate how I felt immediately after my mother died. For
decades, I bottled up this traumatic moment and pushed it completely out of my consciousness to forget about sharing the emotions I felt
with anyone. I have spent the better part of my life burying her death deep
into my memory to shield me from the truth. Yet the hurt and anger all come
rushing back every time I think about the way she died, like it's happening
all over again.

After Uncle Rob delivered the news, I was in complete shock and
denial. I repeatedly went over the details in my mind, hoping for a different
outcome, but the story remained the same. My mother was murdered and
nothing could be done to change this. That evening, I sat in the basement at
the Cottrell's house on an itchy blue couch, staring blankly at an old piano

in disbelief. How could this be happening to me? With a million thoughts running through my head, I eventually passed out from exhaustion.

When the sun hit my face and woke me the next morning, I felt even worse than I did the day before. I was praying it was all just a nightmare, but the reality was setting in. I stayed in bed all day. So many thoughts crossed my mind. Who killed my mother? Who would take care of me? Why would someone kill my mother? Where would I live? What would happen to my brothers?

In an attempt to take my mind off things, Torin started a neighbor-hood-wide game of Hide and Seek. "…18, 19, 20! Ready or not, here I come!" yelled Torin. Out of reluctance to play, I hid in my uncle's boat in the alley on the side of the house. The most crisp breeze came with the wind as I stared into the bluest sky. The temperature in the air was much colder than the day before, and smell of winter marked a shift in the season. Ten minutes passed and I was still lying there, imagining that any minute my mother would pull up in her beige Thunderbird; that this was all a dream. That she would some way, somehow just reappear. I wanted nothing more than to just go home and pretend like none of this was happening.

That night, Aunt Gloria sat me down to let me in on the last conversation she and my mother had the day she dropped me off. She was purposely vague, but informed me that with death threats to our family, my mother couldn't trust anyone. She described to Aunt Gloria how so many people were after her money and her business. If only someone could have protected her. As I listened to Aunt Gloria, I felt sad, but in a different way than before. I could not believe my mother, a young woman with so much love and energy, had been enduring all that uncertainty. It was all so hard to believe.

The wake and funeral were the following weekend. I walked into Swanson's Funeral Home still somewhat in disbelief, but as I got closer to the casket, a feeling of acceptance began to come over me. This was real… all the outrage, confusion, and sorrow I felt came down to this one moment. The moment where life meets death, the moment when we realize that everything that once mattered no longer makes any difference at all. The moment when we recognize that we take our ability to breathe and live for granted. That in just a split second of time, it could all be taken away.

And there she was, looking just as beautiful as she always did. Her energy radiated throughout the entire room, and I could feel it. A discernable sense of peace on her face gave me comfort, and it was that feeling that helped me make it through the day. With so many people in attendance, I tried to be as strong as I could. When it was time to close the casket, I took one final look at her and promised I'd somehow make her proud. But I had to let her go now, and this was the hardest part for me – to know this would be the last time my eyes would see her face. My brothers cried; even without understanding, they could feel the pain that came over me. I walked out of the room right before they closed the casket, and when I did, I realized that just about every person that mattered in my mother's life was in attendance, except for Speedy.

Arthur Carroll, a.k.a. Speedy, was my mother's boyfriend after she split with Ray. He was also a drug dealer, and oddly enough, my mother was robbed and killed outside of HIS apartment. No one had seen or heard from him since the incident. Right at the very moment I was walking away from my mother's casket, an overpowering thought hit me. My gut told me Speedy was the one responsible for my mother's murder. Of all the boyfriends she had, Speedy always gave me this eerie feeling every time he was around. I saw right through his phony gestures and the veil he put over my mother's thoughts. I would watch them together and it was obvious. My mom just liked him too much to notice how manipulating and bogus he was. From the day they met, Speedy tried to control her. Complaints and arguments between the two of them started playing back in my head, and I knew he had to have something to do with her murder!

I thought about it... what were the chances my mother was shot in her back as she was about to get in her car outside of Speedy's apartment? When the police and ambulance arrived at the scene, my mother was already dead.

I know that two police officers questioned Speedy inside of his apartment. After repeated knocks, he finally opened the door. This is how I imagine the conversation went down.

"Hi, I'm officer Steinback. Are you Arthur Carroll?" said the officer as the door opened.

"Uhhhh... yes sir, I am. Is there something I can help you with officer?" Speedy said.

"Do you know a woman by the name of Andrea Murphy?"

"Yes, I know her. Did something happen?"

"Can I ask you when's the last time you've seen Ms. Murphy?" the officer asked as he pulled out a paper and pen.

"Ummm, well, she just left here about thirty minutes ago. Is everything okay? Did something happen?"

"Can you tell me around the exact time she left?" the officer questioned.

"Yeah, it was...well, what time is it now? It's about 9 p.m. now, so I'd say right around 8:30."

"Sir, can you please describe your relationship with Ms. Murphy?"

"Yes, she's my girlfriend. We've been together about a year now. I'm worried man, can you tell me if she's okay?" Speedy said frantically.

"Would you mind if we come inside and take a look?" the officer inquired.

"Yeah, sure come on in. It's getting cold out there. I apologize I didn't offer sooner. Can I get you gentlemen something to drink? Some water? I also have orange juice," Speedy offered.

"No, thank you. Sir, do you own any firearms or have any firearms here in the apartment Mr. Caroll?" said one officer as he started looking around.

"No, I don't. Why do you ask?" Speedy said as he turned toward the kitchen.

"Mr. Caroll, do you remember what you were doing around 8:30 p.m. tonight?"

"Umm, yes... I, uh... I was actually on the phone with my cousin up in Dearborn," Speedy noted.

"Ms. Murphy has been in an accident right outside, and we are told she spent a lot of time at your apartment" the officer stated.

"Accident? Oh shit, what happened? Is she okay? Where is she now? I need to know something, man..."

"No, she's not okay. She's been shot to death, next to her car."

"Oh, my God, what? No! Oh, no... please... that can't be true. She's dead?" Speedy said as he paced back and forth in disbelief.

"Mr. Caroll, do you know of any enemies Ms. Murphy may have had, or someone that might have wanted to get back at her for something?" the officer questioned.

Speedy gathered himself as he digested the question. He wiped his eyes and stood still.

"Enemies? No, no, no. Andrea didn't have none of those."

After searching his home and interviewing him several times, the police cleared him as a suspect. To this day, no one has ever been indicted for the crime. My mother's murder was deemed a random act.

Every incident we each experience on this planet will shape and define who we become. Generally, the depth of each experience advances with age and time. And even though time and age can never exactly prepare you for these unexpected life happenings, they do seem to be more manageable when in play. But some of us are the 'unlucky' ones. Some of us get hit with the hardest bombs quite early on in life, and it is to those people reading this book, that I will take a second to directly speak to.

Understand that your experiences are your armor. Much like studying for a test or practicing for a game, they are moments that prepare us for everything thereafter. And preparation is one of the most important keys to success. There is no successful leader that hasn't embraced the idea of preparation on their journey to the top. As hard as it is to move forward after any traumatizing event, you must try to keep in mind that what you are going through will only make you stronger in the end. These out-of-control moments are forcing a preparation in you that will make you ready for all the things that will come next. So, maybe we aren't the 'unlucky' ones. Instead, we are the ones that faced challenges earlier in life. We are the ones that have been given the opportunity to get ahead of the curve. I didn't realize it at the time, but my mother's death and what I went through as a result of her death, armored me for an accelerated growth far beyond what I could have ever imagined. I wish there was someone who could have told me this when I needed to hear it. You do not have to let the negative things that happen in your life determine your future or define you. Take the bad that happens and use the growth that occurs to enhance your life. Use your experiences as tools to push you forward.

Once the funeral was over and all the well wishes and condolences came to a close, everyone got back to their normal lives. Meanwhile, I was still unsettled, dejected, and frustrated at the entire world that my mother was taken away from me. I couldn't get back to my normal life like everyone else. How was I supposed to explain my mother's death at school? I was gone for a full week, and to my surprise, no one even mentioned it when I finally returned. There were no words of encouragement from any counselors, administrators, teachers, or classmates. Sadly enough, violence and crime happened so often in our environment, no one was really fazed.

After the funeral, my brothers and I would never all live in the same household again. We tried to stay in our house on Santa Rosa Street with my Uncle Skeeter, but that didn't last long because he was still using drugs, and my grandmother was in and out of the hospital. (Uncle Skeeter had used drugs my whole life, but before, we always had our mother and grandmother to take care of us. We had no idea how much the drugs affected his ability to function.) Woo and I ended up moving in with the Cottrells, and Ray went to live with his paternal grandmother. From that point on, there wasn't very much I could do to be there for both of my brothers. Woo and I continued to grow up together, but Ray was being raised in a completely different household. Unfortunately, our bond with him started to fade. I knew I had to figure out a way to survive as we moved forward, so I could set myself up to be there for them later on in life.

> And here is when we see that automatic shift happened in my brain. This is what I was referring to earlier when I mention of a "force of preparation." Every choice I made moving forward held different weight. My immediate objectives in life became clearer. I was changing, and I didn't even know it. I was experiencing an accelerated growth. I had to think ahead and figure things out.

I felt it was my responsibility to be the one to keep it together for my brothers. But what did that mean exactly? Nothing would ever be the same for my family after my mother passed. Even though the Cottrells put a roof over my head, with three meals a day on the table, there was no one I felt I could completely depend on.

The first few months after my mother's death, my grades suffered tremendously. I remember finishing that semester with all Ds and Fs and not caring one bit. I wanted nothing to do with school at that point. I had so many other things on my mind, and it seemed like no one cared about how I felt or what I was going through. All of this caused me to start rebelling.

At the Cottrells, I shared a bed with Torin for months. Brian, Torin's older brother, eventually moved out of his room down into the basement, which left me my own bed, but living under different rules was a challenge. I began to hang around Brian and his older friends regularly. They called themselves the "20/20 Crew." As a result of hanging with them, I started to understand the streets and drug game even more, especially when Brian and his friend, Deon Griffin, started cooking and selling crack cocaine. They would cook it up in the kitchen on Tracey St while Uncle Rob and Aunt Gloria were at work. They took a pot, added some water with baking soda and cocaine, and brought it to a boil. It was called "whipping it." After whipping it, they would let it cool down against ice to turn it into a solid or "rock." Understanding the quick flip method of selling in powder form was huge. Whole bird, half key, quarter key, and 1/8th of a key were quick powder flips. Ounces, half ounces, and 8-balls were cooked up for rock sells. If you had patience, you could cook up an entire kilo and get rich in an instant.

During this time rap music and concerts was still in the ground-breaking stage. With no social media, internet and not much cable television the only way to experience your favorite musician was to catch their show when it came to town. Deon took me to my first ever concert, the Fresh Fest at Cobo Arena, where my love for hip hop exploded! I was mesmerized at thirteen years old watching Run DMC, Whodini and the Fat Boys perform. Rapping and dancing to It's Like That (Run DMC), Five minutes of Funk (Whodini) and Jail House Rap (Fat Boys) will never be forgotten! Fresh Fest had me looking forward to every artist that was due to perform in Detroit the next few years. By the time I turned sixteen I had seen LL Cool J, Eric B & Rakim, Doug E Fresh, Slick Rick, Beastie Boys, Big Daddy Kane and Biz Markie. I still enjoy attending concerts of all genres 30 years later and the feelings that overcame me my first ever concert at Fresh Fest remains the same today!

As the ninth grade approached, I felt like school was completely pointless and could do nothing for me. Little league football ended after eighth grade, and right away I was recruited to play multiple sports as a high school student. Detroit King, Detroit Mumford and Oak Park are the three high schools that relentlessly recruited me to play football. However, I didn't want to dedicate myself to what it took to become an actual student athlete. I was more intrigued with the streets and making money, so I started hanging around Deon and Brian who were selling drugs. Driven by material things, I wanted to be able to buy the latest clothes and have whatever I wanted. Having money in my pocket and a little control over my life caused me to think I was hot stuff. My arrogance would soon lead me to rebel against Aunt Gloria and Uncle Rob's rules: we had to stay on our block if we were outside after dark, no hanging around the older guys, no talking on the phone after 9:00 p.m., and we had a 10:00 p.m. bedtime. I was so fed up with the situation that I went to the Washington family and asked if I could live with them instead. At that point, there were sixteen people living at the Washington house, including me. We were packed into that 1,300 square foot ranch like sardines, and nothing was easy. Taking a shower, using the bathroom, and finding a spot to sleep made the living situation almost unbearable. Sharing a twin bed, with someone different each night, wasn't conducive for proper rest, but I always remained thankful that they welcomed me with open arms. To keep out the way, I stuck with my regular routine of school by day and hanging in the streets by night.

I'll never forget buying my first pair of Air Jordans, and saving up enough money to buy an Elite 50 motor scooter. It was such a good feeling!

And because it felt so good to have that control, academics were not a priority. I started skipping school, never did homework, and developed the sneaky and closed off character traits that I needed to survive in the streets.

About year passed, and Deon was arrested for drug trafficking. Six months prior to Deon's arrest, Brian decided to leave the drug game and got a trucking job. Right around this same time, I received a call from Le Le asking me to stop by Tracey Street. When I pulled up riding my Elite 50 motor scooter, there were cars barricading the entire block. When I finally made my way to the house, I walked in and learned that Brian had died in a trucking accident. My heart fell out of my chest; the only big brother I had ever known was gone. How could this be happening? Just when Brian was getting on the right path, doing the right thing. That's it, now he's gone? I felt like I was being choked; that moment took all the air from my lungs like they were being squeezed to death. I wondered, what was the point anymore? I lost my mom, I lost my dad, I lost Bullet, I lost Ray, and now Brian. I was so sick and tired of this cycle. This just fueled me to stay on the streets. I didn't care anymore. Brian was doing the right thing, and still ended up dead. So, I thought, who cares. I'd do what I wanted when I wanted. I was all alone anyway. I wasn't okay after this.

It is important that I share a detail of my life, which I know has helped me maintain a constant focus. After learning about Brian, I experienced a moment of clarity. As everyone was drinking to cope with their sorrow, as they normally did, I had a thought to see if drinking would help me deal with the pain I was feeling… Everyone else was drinking, so why not? I replayed the first 15 years of my life over and over. I realized that I had never, not even once, used drugs or alcohol. I told myself, at that moment, that I never would. I have maintained this practice well into my 40's. I am sharing this with you because our youth need to know, this is a choice…and whether you are surrounded by drugs and alcohol or only offered it at a party, you have a choice to not get caught up in these life distractions…which can ruin your life and the lives of others. I am not saying this is easy, nor am I trying to preach. I am asking you to think deeply about your future when making these decisions. Anything that distracts you from positivity, consistent growth and future success should always be a HARD NO!

The family was never the same after that. For months, darkness filled the Cottrell house, and I was left to grieve again. Losing Brian hurt me for a long time.

I was home with the Washington's one day when Tyrone and Durinda asked me if anyone in my family had heard from Speedy over the last few years.

"He hasn't contacted any of us since my mom passed," I said.

"Really? I just spoke with him, and he asked how you and your brothers were doing. He mentioned wanting to stop by and see you," Tyrone explained.

A week later, Speedy came by the Washington's house, and when he saw me, he acted like nothing ever happened. He greeted me as if we just saw each other the day before. And that was it… he had nothing notable to say to me, and could hardly look me in the eye. We all sat in the most awkward energy while the Washington's attempted to catch up with him. He conversed with everyone else in the room and avoided any topic of substance.

For me, this encounter fully confirmed that he had a part in my mother's death. And when he walked out the door that night, I was furious that he got away with murder. But time always tells…

A year passed, and I stopped by to visit Uncle Skeeter one Saturday afternoon. After my mother died he left Santa Rosa street and moved into his own place. We sat on the stairs outside the front of his apartment building catching up, and he had a story to tell me.

"Yo, Rob, you remember Speedy's real name?" Uncle Skeeter said as he popped open a bag of chips.

"Of course. Why?" I replied as I reached into my backpack for a box of Lemon Heads.

"What was it?" Uncle Skeeter said.

"Arthur Carroll. What makes you ask?" I responded, still searching through my backpack.

Uncle Skeeter put down the chips and stood up. "Are you serious? That's crazy... Man, I just read an article. You won't fuckin' believe this, man. I just read this article that said Arthur Caroll, in Grand Rapids, shot his wife, same exact way your mother went out, for some insurance money, and he got caught. Sentenced to fifteen years in prison. The dummy even shot himself trying to set it up n' shit like he didn't do the shit."

"What do you mean by insurance money?" I said.

"Speedy took an insurance policy out on your mother, and received some money after she died, and he did the exact same thing to this woman," he said.

I was convinced, "I fuckin' knew it! You gotta be kidding me! He killed my mother! Man, that's unreal! I know that shit for sure now."

I couldn't believe it! When I read the article, there was no denying that he killed my mother. This murder was executed in the exact same manner, but this time he didn't get away with it. The police found evidence at the scene, and he was convicted.

I have become a firm believer in karma. When you do something that you know is wrong, you should just immediately assume that something, be it small or large, will come back around for, and it is only a matter of time. You must live your life the honest way, and do things righteously. It is only then that you will receive all the blessings you deserve. What you do and how you treat others will affect you. Unfortunately, you cannot live in this world alone, and you will need other people to live and to thrive. I cannot stress enough how important it is to treat each person you come across with kindness and gratitude. Someone you meet will have the opportunity to impact your life, and it is through living the right way and treating people the right way that you will be able to utilize the gifts others have to offer to make your life greater.

After short stints of living with the Wright and Bailes families, I ended up moving back to the Cottrell's house the summer approaching my junior year of high school. Mentally, I was all over the place, day-to-day not knowing what was next. I didn't really know where my life was headed. I started riding around with Deon when he returned from jail, listening to his master plan of how he planned to be back on top. Deon, however, would always steer me away from selling drugs myself. He always told me I had a bright future and he would give me whatever I needed, but he never wanted me to be too involved. He always bought me clothes and put money in my pocket, but I always wanted to have a bigger role in the business. I didn't really understand at the time why he believed in me so much. For some reason, he was convinced that I was special and would do all these amazing things in my life one day. I couldn't see it though, so I continued to beg him to let me work in the drug house. I wanted more money, and I wanted to earn it myself.

After several months of begging, he finally broke down and allowed me to do a sit in. One Thursday mid-August, he dropped me and a neighborhood friend, Kevin Wright, to work the night shift on the west side of Detroit at a drug house on Colfax near Tireman. It was about 4:00 a.m. on Friday, and

I was lying on the couch. Right before I was about to doze off, I had a very eerie feeling while staring at the ceiling.

"Kevin, wake me up in an hour. I'll take the next shift and then you can sleep," I said.

I reclined on the couch to get comfortable and passed out. About thirty minutes later, I heard a voice say, "Don't move motha fucka!"

When I opened my eyes, there was a gun pressed to my forehead. Forced into the kitchen, they made Kevin and me lie down on our stomachs, and they put sheets over our entire bodies.

"Count to 100 loud and don't fuckin' move, or I'll kill you!"

But I couldn't just sit there. I kept getting antsy trying to see what they were doing.

I whispered to Kevin, "If they're gonna kill us anyway, why not go down with a fight?"

Kevin kept telling me to stop moving and keep counting, but I didn't listen. Bam! I was hit in the back of my head with a gun handle.

"Shut up! If you move again motha fucka, you're dead!"

"35, 36, 37, 38…," and suddenly things went silent.

I slowly pulled my head from under the sheet, and saw that they were gone. And so were all of the drugs, guns, and money that sat on the dining table.

That was an eye-opening experience for me. From that day forward, I never went into another drug house ever again. God stepped in that time, and I was lucky enough to walk out alive. A month later, one of our friends who worked for Deon was shot and killed in the exact same situation, which continued to confirm how fortunate I was that morning on Colfax.

When September came around, I started school with a better attitude. A buddy of mine, Kenny Fenton, who played football was complaining about how sucky the team was last year, and suggested that I join the team to help them out. Everyone knew me as one of the swiftest running backs in little league. I was also known for my defensive back skills, so he knew I could play. He even got the coaches on board with the idea, and a day later they were trying to recruit me. I wasn't interested at first, but with Deon supporting me, I didn't feel compelled to be in the streets making money.

I joined the Mumford High School Football team my junior year, and believe it or not, my coaches and friends were right. I helped the Mustangs win more games that season than any other time before. Being a part of the team that year rerouted the entire course of my life. From my participation, I gained the support and felt the sense of community I needed to excel not only in school, but as a growing adolescent. When the season ended, I tried out for the basketball team. It was then that I learned basketball was my passion. However, my natural athletic ability made me a better football player.

My involvement in the sports programs that year led me to meet some new friends and mentors that I have kept in touch with long after high school. My little league coach, Coach Fig, and best friend, Aaron Hayden, motivated me and kept me involved with football. Aaron had the work ethic of Kobe Bryant, and was a living example of how consistent practice paid off. He was a fearless and tough competitor, who was always prepared for the moment. I admired this about him and set out to do the same.

Oronde Taliaferro, Ra Murray, and Dwayne Lowery were friends I met through little league football and basketball, and who also helped steer me in a completely different direction. Memories at Oronde's and Murray's houses are unforgettable. Murray and I became the best of friends and were inseparable. The more I hung around positive and progressive people, the more I wanted to stay away from the streets. I know today that my coaches, Robert Lynch and Venius Jordan, were God sends. Essentially, they turned my entire life around. Coach Jordan took me under his wing during my junior year, and he did everything in his power to keep me focused on academics and doing the right thing. I do not know where I'd be today without his reliable guidance.

The summer before my tenth-grade year, a girl named Deanna, who I went to school with, became my girlfriend. Loved by everyone we knew, she was the most genuine and caring soul. Unlike me, Deanna came from a very big family. She has a sister, Angie, who was cool, and many aunts and uncles… scary, body-builder uncles. Deanna and I were head over heels in love. I mean we were inseparable. As if seeing each other every day during school wasn't enough, we found additional time to spend together by skipping class. We became the best of friends, and she was closer to me than anyone ever was.

Her family was very involved in her life, which made it difficult for us to have a committed relationship. Their support took a complete turn when Deanna was unable to maintain her focus and drive with school. Her family tried to force Deanna to stay away from me, but we were so in love that nothing was going to stop the feelings we carried for one another. Ignoring her family's wishes, we continued to sneak around throughout high school. Her mother tried everything she could to keep us apart. Eventually, her mother realized there was nothing she could really do to control the situation, so she finally gave in our senior year.

Because I spent so much time in the streets my ninth-grade year, I was behind academically. After my junior year, I realized I was in danger of not graduating on time. I had to take four summer school classes prior to my senior year to put me back on the trajectory to graduate. If I didn't pass these classes, I would not be eligible to play football or basketball my senior year. That fact alone gave me the incentive I needed to finish summer school.

During that time, Marsha Keys, an economics teacher at Mumford High, saw my determination and regularly encouraged me. Because she understood what I was going through both mentally and emotionally, her approach to helping me with school was different. She took the time to notice that I was acting out amongst my peers because I wasn't getting the attention

I needed at home. With my grandmother still in hospital and no consistent male figure, I was seeking acceptance in the wrong ways. Through our chats and just spending time in the classroom, we developed a strong relationship. Marsha's super cool and caring personality prompted me to quickly buy into her wisdom. She was never focused on my athletic ability, but beat in my head the importance of respecting women and getting an education. To keep me on track, and off the street, she rewarded me with incentives through academic success. I would continue to challenge myself to do the right things in order to not let her down. It wasn't long before she became a mother figure for me. Today, I call her my Godmother.

It took a very strong mind set to overcome some of the early circumstances of my life. The temptation of wanting to sell drugs to make money instead of continuing to play sports and be around positive people was always a struggle for me. I felt like I was being torn between two different lifestyles. But the constant threat of death or jail helped me to make better choices. Even when the allure of the streets reeled me back in, the positive circle of people I gained through sports helped me stay focused. All I went through during those years of my life shut me down and forced me to not trust anyone. I was living behind a mask. No one knew about my internal fight but God. I controlled the perception others had of me by pretending to always be okay, when in reality, that was far from the truth. When I left school, I still had to go home and deal with my sad dysfunctional reality. My aloneness.

God always answered with essential guidance through each of my experiences, and a blanket of angels seemed to be always watching over me. Whenever it was time for me to understand, God provided a way. Good or bad, I always gained a lesson. There is literally nothing else that can explain how I escaped being two seconds or three steps away from death and jail, but God. My mother's spirit also kept me going. I would always think about her smile. Everything she instilled in me aided my ability to become more than anyone could have ever imagined.

By the end of my senior year, I was an All-City, All-State football player, and I led the metro Detroit area in interceptions. Because of this, I was recruited and offered scholarships by several Division I universities to play football. The entire Mid-American Conference (MAC) offered me scholarships. People thought I was going to be the next NFL super star. I ended up committing to and signing with Eastern Michigan University. All I had to do to officially qualify for the scholarship offer was pass the ACT with a test score of 18 or higher. There was nothing I could do at that point to properly prepare for the ACT. I took the test several times, but continued to fall a few points shy of the required score, and just like that, my scholarship offer fell right through my hands. It was too good to be true; things were falling into place perfectly, and then bam! My inability to score high enough on the ACT test changed it all. I immediately began to weigh my options. I would fall under Proposition 48 if I still decided to attend Eastern Michigan.

In the early 90's, eighty seven percent of Prop 48 athletes were African American. After years of research it was found that there was a definite correlation between socioeconomic background and ACT/SAT scores in the black community. Prop 48 crushed thousands of black athletes' dreams about receiving an athletic scholarship to attend college. The NCCA faced years of scrutiny behind this biased rule, which created the NCAA's current sliding scale for academic qualification. This change has helped thousands of student-athletes to qualify to receive an athletic scholarship. Had the sliding scaling been around today, I would've played football for the Eastern Michigan Eagles!

I was so disappointed with the results, and my coaches were as well. But Coach Venius Jordan was determined to get me to the next level. He refused to let my potential go to waste because of one test that the Detroit Public School system never properly prepared students for.

My senior season of basketball included the signature win of my high school basketball career, a victory over Cooley High School, coached by the legendary Ben Kelso, in the district championships. We were huge underdogs playing against a perennial powerhouse, and we beat them in a close game. Ironically, my best friend Ra Murray gave us the biggest assist of the game.. from the stands. With 12 seconds left and down by one, we intentionally fouled a player with a low free throw percentage. As Ra sat in the stands behind our bench, he noticed that Cooley sent the wrong player to the line. Ra immediately got our attention and brought to light that a better player was shooting. When we pointed this out to the officials, Cooley got a technical foul. Keynon Myers swished both free throws for us to seal the game. It was an amazing moment, and to this day, it is still one of my favorite athletic memories. I was also very proud of my defensive performance that day, as I held Walter Wilson, who was averaging 19 points a game, to a mere four points.

After a solid basketball season and continuing frustrations with the ACT exam, Coach Jordan reached out to Kevin Porter, a former NBA player and head coach at the historically black college, Central State University (CSU) in Wilberforce, Ohio. Knowing that I really wanted to play basketball, he pitched me to Coach Porter, with hopes that he had an open scholarship for the upcoming school year. Coach Porter had already given out the allotted scholarships for the year, but he was interested to see if I could still be an asset to the team. After watching me play, he put an offer on the table. If I decided to attend Central State, I would need to earn the scholarship by showing I could excel academically and be an asset to the team…all after sitting out of any basketball related activities my freshman season.

I ended up taking Coach Porter's offer and went to Central State University to play basketball. I would be the FIRST member of my family to ever graduate high school and go to college.

Chapter Three

AGAINST ALL ODDS

I can only imagine how proud my mother was when she looked down on that moment. For many people, attending college after high school is a standard progression in the maturation of life. But for me, and where I came from, it defied normality. In fact, more than half of the kids I grew up with never made it to college. The cost of college alone made it so far out of reach, students were reluctant to apply. Even with the odds stacked against me, and the personal losses I suffered in my life, I somehow managed to get into college and land a scholarship to play basketball. I would not be another grim statistic.

There I was packing up the few belongings I had, and on my way to CSU. That was a huge moment for my family, and an inspiration for the generations after me. But I didn't suddenly become immune to the cycle of life. A month before I went to school, one of my uncles, Uncle Sonny, died of liver failure, due to an excessive drinking habit. Unbeknownst to me, I was one of the beneficiaries of Uncle Sonny's life insurance policy, so I received $5,000 after his death. With that money, I purchased my very first car, a white 1985 Ford Mustang.

When the week came for me to leave for school, I had no one to come with me. Originally, my Uncle Rob had plans to drive me to school and help me get settled, but at the last minute, his plans changed because of work. Again, there I stood alone, having to navigate the unknown. I was initially upset that Uncle Rob couldn't take me to CSU, but then I thought about how painful it could have been for him to drop me off at college after his own son's life was ripped away from him without the chance for a future. Though I wanted him there with me, I was kind of glad he couldn't make it.

Fortunately, Trent Mitchell, a classmate from high school, was also attending CSU and needed a ride. At 10:00 p.m. on a quiet Tuesday, we packed up the Mustang. That was the first time I ever left the Detroit area in my entire life.

When I glanced out of my rear-view mirror, a heavy feeling came over me. As I started the car, I reflected on all I was leaving behind. So much had happened in my first seventeen years. Even though I understood the magnitude of it all, I hadn't completely grasped the accomplishment and possibility that waited ahead. A whole new world was opening for me.

Of course, before I got out of Detroit, I had to see Deanna. Through it all, Deanna was always there in the background of everything that went on with me. I didn't realize it at the time, but Deanna played a major role in helping me get to this point in my life. She was the first female I trusted after my mother died, making us very close. We had a solid friendship before we started dating, and the relationships I witnessed within her entire family showed me what it meant to be loyal and affectionate.

I'll never forget how I felt when I stood at the side door of her house on Pennington Street to say goodbye. It was as if we would never see each other again. Tears fell from my eyes as we hugged one last time. Change is inevitable. I had grown accustomed to dealing with constant change at an early age, but I had never experienced the heartache of having to leave someone like this ever in my life. Although it was difficult for me to take this next step, I knew it had to be done.

We arrived at CSU around 7:00 a.m. the next day. Upon our arrival, the first two students we met, who are still good friends, were Rob Mack and Hugh Douglass, from Mansfield, Ohio. Trent and I were assigned to be roommates in Page Hall, an upperclassman honors dorm. How we got into Page Hall still remains a mystery, but we were more than satisfied. Our room was on the second floor. It was about 300 square feet with bunk beds. We unloaded the car and got settled to prepare for our 9:00 a.m. orientation the next day.

When I graduated high school, Coach Jordan advised me to major in education. He believed this would allow me to start a teaching and coaching career in the Detroit Public School system. And that's what I did. From the moment I stepped foot on the CSU campus, I knew exactly what I wanted to do after college. Because of this, I wasted no time, and always saw further ahead than my counterparts. Transitioning to college life was relatively simple after I was there a few days. My childhood had prepared me to adjust and learn on the fly. It was, however, a little tough getting used to the fact that I wouldn't be playing sports for a whole year.

The CSU football program won the national championship in 1990, a year before. People started to get to know me on campus, and some of the football players learned about how talented I was on the field; they understood that leading the city of Detroit in interceptions was a very difficult thing. When they saw my highlight footage, they wanted me to join the team. Football was the initial reason I was recruited by so many different schools. It was obvious that I had a sheer undeniable talent on the field. However, I didn't love football the way I loved basketball. Even when I was being recruited by those various universities, I always knew in my heart it wasn't what I fully wanted. Yes, if I would've had a high enough ACT score, I would have surely accepted a full ride at Eastern Michigan to play football, but I was glad I was going to get the opportunity to hoop at CSU.

When I was offered to join the CSU football program, by Hall of Fame coach Billy Joe my freshman year. I was flattered but declined. My heart belonged to basketball, and the following year I would get to play. To pass the time and stay sharp, I decided to get involved in an intramural basketball team on campus. When I could, I would sit in on the team's practices to assess where my talent would rank among the guys next season. The time couldn't go by quickly enough before I got the opportunity to be on that court under the guidance of former NBA point guard, Coach Kevin Porter. Every single day, I added something basketball related into my schedule. I continued to work on my game throughout the school year and summer to prepare myself for next season. I LOVE the game of basketball like no other.

After the first two weeks of school, I drove back home. I missed Deanna so much and also wanted to check on my grandmother. As soon as I got off of Interstate 75, I went straight to Deanna's house. I had never been so happy to see someone in my life. There were no words when our eyes met for the first time again. I hugged her so tight, and then proceeded to tell her everything that happened in my first few weeks of school. When some of my family found out that I was in Detroit, they were disappointed I came back so soon, thinking I wasn't giving the transition a chance. I explained that I was doing fine at Central but just got a little homesick.

My grandmother was elated to see me.

"Am I looking at the most beautiful woman in the world?" I said as I strutted into her hospital room with a bouquet of flowers.

She gasped, "Is that my little Chick. Boy, what are you doin' here? You're supposed to be at school!"

"I wanted to come check on my favorite girl," I said with a grin.

"No, you wanted to check on your girl, Deanna," she laughed.

"No, I'm here to check on my only girl, Annie Mae Pierson," I said as I sat on her bed and wrapped my arm around her. We shared a laugh, and then I continued, "So how are you grandma?"

"I'm fine, baby, don't you worry about me. I want you to just focus on those grades and staying at that school, and making it through; cause you're the one to do it. I'll be just fine if you can do that one thing for me. Don't be running back here and hanging around the thugs in the neighborhood. You stay far away from that stuff. You are on the right track and don't look back. If you can stay away from here, you're gonna do some big things, Chick. We believe in you. Me, your brothers, Uncle Skeeter… your mom. You know, I used to tell your mama all the time you were special. There's something about that heart of yours, and your mama had it, too. You just keeping pushing forward, and you will find your place, I just know it. And don't let no one stop you either. We're gonna hear about that name up in heaven. ROB MURPHY."

"You're not going to heaven anytime soon. So, I guess I have time," I said with a smile.

Seeing my grandmother brought up the suppressed emotions of my mother being gone. I wished so badly that I could share these moments and all the growth I had experienced with my mom. Returning home was a nice break for me. It was refreshing to check on my brothers and realize that leaving was the best thing I could have ever done for them. For them to see me graduate from high school, and actually go off to college, reassured them that they could achieve the same. I was their hero, and that was all the motivation I needed to get back on Interstate 75. I left that Sunday morning recharged and ready to return to CSU.

Being in college and living on campus gave me a sense of freedom I hadn't experienced before. There were so many things I no longer had to worry about. This was the first time, in a way, I could actually be my age. I wasn't worried about where I would rest my head or what I would eat, who would pay the bills, or how my family was doing. It was freeing to finally understand what it felt like to just live for me. I did, however, need money for things here and there, so I learned how to shoot dice. Eventually, I met Mike Frazier, Houston's and CSU's finest gambler, who taught me how to become one of the best dice rollers in the history of CSU. Every weekend, I would make a decent sum of cash gambling with other students on campus.

As my freshman year continued, I began to gain popularity. My stylish wardrobe and gold chains gained attention at every party and event I attended. Being from Detroit held lots of clout with students from other places. Detroit guys were known to be the trendiest and the toughest. I fit right into that mode and took full advantage of the Detroit reputation.

As for Deanna and I, we started to lose touch. Our lives were growing in different directions, and eventually the relationship faded out. There wasn't any particular event that caused us to break up, but time and distance made it inevitable that we separated. I think both of us just naturally started experiencing new things and meeting different people. Deanna also decided not to attend college right away, so everything that I was going through she didn't totally relate to at the time. Our commonalities were no longer shared. It bothered me when we decided to let things go. But just as it always does at the most perfect time, life stepped in to ease the heartache.

On a Tuesday, as I was rushing to get to my most dreaded anthropology class, I ran into the most beautiful girl I had ever seen. Time literally slowed down, just as it does in every movie when the young boy unexpectedly bumps into the gorgeous popular girl on campus. She completely took my breath away. She had the most perfect tan complexion, with sharp features and long, straight black hair. After staring at her, for what felt like twenty minutes, I snapped out of it, and there she was saying, "I'm Tracye, and you are?"

By the end of my first semester, Tracye Givens was my girlfriend. She was a year older, popular, had her own car, and lived off campus. I believe she only looked my way because we met in a building where upperclassmen courses were held, and she likely assumed I was older. Luckily, my age made no difference after she already fell for me. I had little to offer Tracye, but we had the most exciting relationship. I ended up failing anthropology that semester. Turns out, I was in an upperclassmen course, making it difficult, in addition to the fact that I had no interest in it. Despite this, I was still in good enough academic standing to officially become a member of the Marauder basketball team the following season, and that's what mattered to me most. As I packed up my dorm room to depart for summer vacation all I could visualize was returning to campus for a tremendous sophomore year academically and athletically.

When I finally arrived back in Detroit, my entire block was waiting to see me. I was excited to be home for the summer, ready to spending time with friends and family. As I turned onto Tracey St. I could hear music a block away. Torin loved to shake the neighborhood from his boomin' system in the trunk of his Monte Carlo. The "old school" classic was a beauty. It was sky blue, had chrome Dayton spoke wheels, with piped out blue leather seats. A picture of the Tasmanian Devil was stitched inside both head-rest. After catching up with everyone Torin ask me did I want to ride with him to grab something to eat.

"Murph, let's go grab something to eat" ask Torin.

"Ok cool, I can use a bite" I replied

"Do you want to drive my car? This boy rides smooth" Torin suggested.

"Nah, I'm good man. I just got off the highway so I'm going to ride shot gun, relax and enjoy your banging music."

Five minutes later we pulled into the McDonalds on 7 mile and the Lodge blasting Down with the King by Run DMC.

"Welcome to McDonalds, go ahead with your order when you're ready".

"Let me have a #2 add cheese and a #8, both with Cokes."

"Your total is $9.62 please pull around."

As we were waiting for our food, a brown Pontiac 6000 pulled up four feet from us. The back door of the car slowly opened and out came the barrel of a gun pointing directly at me with bandana covered face.

"Get the fuck out" was the yell. Before I could think I jumped over Torin's lap (as he was receiving the food through the drive through window). I could hear the cashier screaming as I attempted to jump through her window but within a split second I decided to drop on the side of the car, and run towards the back of McDonalds.

"Hurry up, get the fuck out before I kill you Motherfucker"!

Three seconds later, Pop! Pop! Pop! I thought Torin was a goner! I took a peak back and could see Torin running to catch up with me. I was relieved to see him, but as he got closer he started to limp.

"Murph, help me! I think he shot me. I feel this burn in the back of my leg near my butt" I stopped to help him and we realized Torin had been shot from the blood that became visible. Ironically, two friends Quincy and Bally happened to be in the drive through directly behind us and witnessed the entire incident. They immediately called 911 to get medical help but we couldn't afford to wait so they drove us to the emergency room to get immediate attention. We later found out there was an undercover police officer ordering food inside McDonalds as this was happening. He got on his police radio to call in what was happening. Fifteen minutes later the carjacker was caught and arrested after shooting at the police and crashing Torin's Monte Carlo a few miles away. The following day I visited 1300 Beaubien police station downtown Detroit to see if I could identify the shooter in a police lineup.

"Do you see the person who shot your cousin Torin in this lineup?" ask the officer

"Yes, Number 6, that's him! I'm positive, #6 for sure. He's the one who jumped out the car and pointed the gun at my face and made us get out of the car!"

It was a scary start to my summer vacation. I thank GOD that Torin and I both survived that day. I knew my priorities for the summer would be spending countless hours in the gym to enhance my basketball skills and staying completely out of harm's way!

Competing in the legendary St. Cecilia basketball league in Detroit, with some of the best college and NBA players, was competitive, challenging and fun. After the great games we'd hang out in the parking lot before deciding on a place to compete in John Madden. Because of mutual friends, Jalen Rose and I became pretty cool over the summer. J Rose was one of the best high school players the state of Michigan has ever produced. He had just completed his freshman year at University of Michigan, as part of the legendary Fab Five. This talented group of freshmen led Michigan to the national championship game, and Jalen was a huge contributor to their success. However, I will always remember, that even though he was a phenomenal talent, he remained humble and just one of the guys.

Prairie Street off of Tireman with Damon, Fred, Gee and the crew became the hangout spot. Madden and dice games became our daily routine after basketball. J Rose was a pretty good Madden player, loved playing with the Giants while calling everyone TOD (turnover on downs) during those battles. When we decided to "shake em up, shake em up, shake em up, shake em (Ice Cube voice)" I always left Prairie St with everyone's money!

After a safe, productive summer in Detroit with friends and family, I was ready to go back to CSU to make an impact on the court. When I stepped back on campus, I had a new roommate. His name was Donte Baker, and we shared a room in the best dorm at Central, Lane Hall. Donte was from Detroit and attended Mumford so we had some familiarity with each other. Things were looking good heading into my sophomore year. At that point,

I was pretty well known at CSU, and Tracye and I were still dating. I was particularly excited about attending my first team meeting.

"Identify and understand your role. Do your job at a high level," were the instructions Coach Porter gave to start off the meeting.

The energy in the gym was electric, and the other players were welcoming and supportive. We started off with a good camaraderie, which is vital to a great season. Coming in as a sophomore put me ahead of the incoming freshmen, because I already had relationships with most of the guys.

"I look forward to a progressive season with you all. Now, please head to the locker room and suit up for your first strength and conditioning workout with Coach Boyd," Coach Porter announced to close the meeting.

Right then, we all looked around at each other totally confused. We were unaware that we were actually starting conditioning that very day, so it was a bit of a shock. But after Coach's command, we immediately got up to change clothes, and headed back to the court where we were in for a rude awakening.

Coach Boyd was not playing around with us. "Suicide drills from the first line all the way down the court. Last one to finish gives me ten push-ups! Go!"

Sneakers squeaking against the floors and deep breaths were all you could hear as the whistle sounded. For the next two hours, we went through an entire conditioning series. None of the team was prepared for that intensity. By the end of the series, we were out of the gym and on the track to run laps. Two laps in, and I couldn't go any further. I completely collapsed to my knees, and started vomiting. Some of my teammates stopped to help me, but I was definitely embarrassed. I wasn't a high school athlete any longer.

"Great job on your first day of work outs. Today is the hardest day. Now get some rest and be here same time tomorrow," Coach Boyd said enthusiastically.

When I finally got back to my dorm, I was beat. I hadn't even unpacked, but I was so tired that all I could do was go to sleep. It was obvious to me then that things would be a lot different this year, now that I was on the team.

For the entire first month of school, we had class from 9:00 a.m. – 3:00 p.m., and pre-season workouts right after from 4:00 – 6:00 p.m. I hardly had time for anything but homework and sleep. By October, official practices began. Workouts were moved to the mornings, and practice ran every day from 4:00 – 6:00 p.m. Coach Porter began to join us in the gym more frequently. The feeling in the air shifted when Coach Porter walked into the gym for practice. Suddenly we were all in competition mode, knowing that we were each fighting for a starting spot. Our practices consisted of heavy conditioning and learning his pro-style NBA offense. Coach Porter loved guys who could score with the ball, so not being a natural scorer, I had to work extra hard to gain his attention. He was a hands-on coach who wasn't afraid to yell and challenge his players in order to get the best out of them. The assistant coaches aided him in practice, but it was always clear who was in charge. He held us all accountable for each role and position we had on the team. I think that is what I enjoyed most about his coaching style. His heavy involvement was key to our program. When he talked, he commanded the attention of the entire room. That was the kind of energy and leadership he possessed.

Coach Porter was a successful former NBA player who had many life challenges. His experiences with drug abuse throughout his tenure in the NBA cost him a lot of money, and a Hall of Fame basketball career. Coach Porter and I immediately hit it off and formed a close bond. We'd play one-on-one before practice, and he'd always find a way to cheat to win, or quit before the game was actually over, if I was close to winning. But most importantly, despite all of the basketball knowledge he shared with us, his major mission was to teach us important things about life. I'll never forget the countless talks I had with him in his office, most of which were about more than just basketball. He shared many great stories with me about his tenure playing in the NBA, the good and bad along with regrets. He wasn't solely interested in just having a good season. He wanted to inspire us to become responsible men who made smart choices. He was so invested in each of us personally, and always made us feel like we were a family.

It was Halloween of 1993, and eight years ago on that day, my mother was murdered. She would have only been thirty-seven years old, and in the prime of her life. I always think about my mom profoundly on this date, so after practice I decided to visit the mall to do some shopping. My mom loved to shop, and though I rarely went, when I did, I could remember what it felt like to be around her. Walking through a department store took me back to running through clothing racks and playing Hide and Seek with my cousins and friends, while my mom and her best friend Cookie tried to put together the latest styles. As I walked around Elder-Beerman's I imagined her shopping around, until I was interrupted by a phone call (I was one of the only students on campus with a cell phone at that time). When I picked up my cell, it was Aunt Gloria. She called to tell me that my grandmother passed away. It was the exact same day. All I could think about was the last conversation I had with her. I broke out in tears right there in Elder-Beerman's, but the crying didn't last long before a smile came to my face. I could hear my grandmother's voice saying, "We're gonna hear about that name up in heaven! ROB MURPHY." I guessed I better get to work so I could make that happen. A week later in Detroit, a small private funeral attended by about thirty people followed the passing of my grandmother. Of course, I was saddened by her death, but I felt more relived that she was out of the hospital and didn't have to fight anymore. The pain was over. I believe it was by design that my grandmother died on the exact same day my mother passed eight years prior. I think she decided on that specific day to let go.

A few days after the funeral, it was time for our first game. We were surely prepared, but I was still nervous as I walked out to a fully packed house. I sat eagerly on the bench, waiting for my name to be called to get in the game. Unsure of exactly what to expect, I jumped right in when my name was called, and did just as I was supposed to. I "played my role." Moments after I stepped on the court, I had a steal, and was fouled. From there, I made both free throws, and it was smooth sailing from then on. I played point guard, and Coach Porter expected flawless basketball from that position. I could not make a single mistake.

Right after the holidays, we were midway into the season. Our first game back from the break, we played Urbana University, and I had one of the worst games of my college career. I made the biggest mistake I've ever made on the court. We had an opportunity to win the game, and I took a bad shot coming out of a timeout, which caused us to lose. I honestly didn't remember the play Coach Porter drew up in the huddle, which was inexcusable. Coach Porter scolded me so harshly that I had tears in my eyes. I didn't do anything he told me to do in the huddle, and I knew that it was my fault.

The next day during practice, he continued to chastise me, and I was still frustrated from the day before. I already felt like shit for forgetting the play and taking a stupid shot, and I didn't need any more reminders. It got so bad that I couldn't take his voice any longer. I stopped in the middle of practice, threw down the ball, and looked right at him before going off.

"Stop yelling at me! I'm not you! I'm not an NBA player, so stop expecting me to be as good as you. I'm not as good as you were! You need to understand that!"

That day, I was kicked out of the gym and held accountable for my outburst, regardless of whether I had a point or not. That was also the moment Coach Porter changed how he coached me. Instead of only being vocal when mistakes were made, he acknowledged when things were done right as well. This gave me more confidence, and in turn made me a more effective player for our team. My sophomore season had a lot of ups and downs. But I learned a great deal about basketball, and even more about myself. I started in a few games, but never became a full-time starter. I played a decent number of minutes, and I understood my role on the court. When the season came to a close, I was ready for the time away from basketball.

Chapter Four

WHO GON' STOP ME

fter investing all your energy envisioning what you want your life to be, it's an amazing feeling when everything you imagined starts to fall into place. Most people make the mistake of thinking, "Man, if only this would happen, life would be so much better," without calculating the added headaches that success can bring. Like the Notorious B.I.G. once said, "Mo' Money, Mo' Problems." As a cocky young man coming into my own, I learned very quickly that life doesn't get simpler just because you're reaching your goals, it actually gets more complicated.

Heading into my third year of college, nothing could be going more right for me. I was playing collegiate basketball on scholarship, I had great friends, and I was dating one of the most popular girls in school. As my Junior year began, I was getting more attention on campus than ever before. There wasn't a corner we could turn without being noticed. I was the guy would could relate and communicate with everyone on campus. And while all the attention and perks of being an athlete were great, there was definitely a downside.

As a twenty-one year old young man, it was only natural that the attention I got from the girls on campus was intriguing. My life was turning out to be a Jay-Z classic, *Girls, Girls, Girls.* And truthfully, what guy wouldn't want a bunch of pretty women throwing themselves at him? It was so difficult for me to shy away from the temptation that I ended up cheating on my girlfriend Tracye. When I was able to get away with it, that one time turned into three times… then five times… and before I could stop myself, I was caught in a web of lies. There was no way I should have continued to be in a committed relationship. But I couldn't just end it. I still wanted to be with her even though I was messing around with other girls.

I believe that many young men, particularly athletes, will experience this exact predicament. It's as if you are living two different lives at once. Both very appealing, but they're not supposed to coincide. And you don't want to lose either one. Nothing can prepare you for these moments. The key here is to be honest with yourself, and then be honest with who you are dealing with.

Needless to say, my relationship with Tracye had an unpleasant ending, especially when her friends got involved. In the process, however, I ended up building a bond with her best friend, Keisha Foster. Keisha and I remained friends even after Tracye and I broke up. It's through Keisha that I ended up meeting Marlene Foster, her cousin from Dayton, Ohio. Marlene was a former CSU student who would always come to campus to hang out and go to parties. Ironically Marlene and Tracye were acquaintances because they both were from Dayton. Marlene and I instantly hit it off. We could talk for hours at a time. Before I knew it, what started off as a really good friendship eventually turned into a serious relationship. I didn't plan for this to happen, but our personalities really clicked, and being friends before dating allowed us to really get to know each other.

Throughout the summer before my junior year, I drove from Detroit to visit Marlene in Dayton a few times, but my main focus was training and working out so I could compete for the starting point guard position next season. I stayed consistent and challenged myself even more than the previous summer. I basically lived at the Tinal and Herman Gardens Recreation centers. My good friend, Oronde, who was going to be a senior at Wayne State University, joined me in daily workouts. We mostly worked on ball handling and shooting. Twice a week, we'd compete in the summer league at St. Cecilia, and play pick up whenever there was a good run. By the end of the summer, I'd saved enough money from gambling to buy a 1987 Mazda 626. It was tricked out with sweet "Star Rims" and an incredible sound system. When I arrived back at CSU for my junior year, I felt like the big man on campus. My kinsman Lance, who was in his senior year at CSU, was looking for a roommate, so I decided that would be the perfect opportunity for me to move off campus.

A new season was on the horizon, and we were all recharged from the break. That year, a highly recruited incoming freshman class would be joining us, and our possibility of winning was greater than it had ever been at CSU. There was no better time to be a part of CSU basketball. Everyone was anticipating a great season.

I competed to the best of my ability and even stayed in the gym practicing extra hours to improve, but it just wasn't enough. Coach Porter wasn't satisfied with my inability to score. With the season right around the corner, he told me I wasn't ready. I know now that part of my desire to start stemmed from having a big ego at the time. I wanted to live up to my reputation as the big man on campus. But you learn as time goes on that these superficial things don't really matter. Many guys see these decisions as personal setbacks, when in fact, things are put in place for the TEAM to move forward the best way possible. Individual goals should never outweigh what is best for a TEAM. Coach Porter did what he knew was best for the TEAM to succeed, regardless of what I wanted. He saw a bigger picture that I couldn't see.

The season was in full swing, and although I wasn't deemed the top point guard, I ended up starting quite a few games. Traveling to Detroit to play against Alabama State at the State Fairgrounds was supposed to be a highlight for me. Once the schedule came out, I circled this game in my mind. It was the first time my family and friends were all there to support me. I was eager and ready to show off for everyone who came out.

After the starting five took the floor for a while, I started rolling my wrists and ankles so I could stay warm. I waited… and waited… and waited some more. Finally, right before halftime, Coach Porter put me in the game. I bolted onto the court. The crowd roared when I hit the floor, and I was at ease now that my family would see me in action. But two minutes later, Coach subbed me out. I jogged back to the bench completely confused. Why the hell did he yank me? I was barely in the game! My confusion slowly turned to anger. But when I looked over at him, he didn't say a word. Coach never put me back in the rest of the game, and we lost.

After the game, I couldn't face my family. I was so embarrassed that they all showed up, and I only played two measly minutes. Looking back now, I realize that I missed the bigger picture again. Coach Porter could obviously see that my head wasn't completely in the game. With my family and friends in the stands, he knew I wanted to perform well, not really for the benefit of our team, but for my own satisfaction. I felt that we lost that game because I didn't get to play, but I understand now that I wasn't in the right headspace to properly perform to help lead us to victory.

Away from the court, life was still good. My relationship with Marlene continued to grow, and her parents, grandparents, cousins, sisters, and brother all welcomed me into their family. This was the first time I felt like I had a genuine home away from home. I was invited to every family event, her parents came to my games, and they always made sure I had everything I needed during my time in school. Dating Marlene allowed me to experience things I didn't experience growing up. I credit the Foster family for helping me have such a successful junior and senior year at CSU. I was more focused academically than I ever before. My grades reflected the positive relationship that Marlene and I had. This was the girl I could see myself marrying.

Although my personal life was going smoothly, right before the summer before my senior year, I found out that I needed to take three summer classes to graduate that would not be offered at CSU in the fall. The pressure was on. If I didn't pass each one, I wouldn't graduate. I enrolled in two of those classes that summer with one of the most difficult professors in the history of CSU, Dr. Howard. I'm proud to say that with a lot of focus and hard work, I passed with a B in each class. The third class, I took at Wright State University in Fairborn, Ohio, which was known at the time as "White State" because of the racism toward blacks that went on there in the late 80's. The education class I took had thirty-two students, and I was the ONLY black student in the class. I felt very uncomfortable in this setting, as it was something I had never experienced before.

While I was taking this class, the O.J. Simpson trial was going on. He is the former Hall of Fame running back accused of murdering his ex-wife and her friend. Simpson is black and the victims were white. The trial captivated the entire country, and caused a rift between the black people who proclaimed his innocence and the white folks who swore he was guilty. I will never forget what happened when the decision was reached while I was in class. On October 3, 1995, as the judge read the verdict, all thirty-one students turned and stared at me. It was the first time I encountered being singled out because of my skin color. Words cannot describe the distinct feeling I had. Through all of the tough times, I had never felt this type of discomfort. It made me aware that these folks saw me as different, because of the color of my skin.

The advice from my high school coach held much more meaning as my senior year approached. Even though I followed the plan to major in education as he suggested, there was always a small glinting hope that I could somehow become good enough to have a professional career playing basketball.

The reality is, the majority of guys don't ever make it, so having an attainable career goal is very important. Once I squashed my hoop dreams, I started to feel overwhelmed about my future. I knew for sure then that there was no way I would make it playing basketball professionally, so I really had to start understanding how to put my education major into action. Time was ticking. I had one more summer of freedom before things were about to get real.

By far, the most memorable part of that summer was having my brothers visit me at CSU for a month. It gave us a chance to rebuild a bond that was broken. After I went to school, we didn't spend much time together, and our lives continued to move in different directions. So, that time with them meant a lot to me. Life was challenging for all three of us, and I had left them in Detroit to get my education and better my future. I wanted them to know they could do the same. In between trips to the movies and dining hall, I emphasized how imperative it was for them to be educated. No matter what we did, I made sure I steered the conversation back to that idea. I wanted to expose them to college life, and inspire them to believe they could get there. When they got back on the road to Detroit, I needed to leave a lasting impression.

After my brothers left, the summer flew by. During my senior season, our team was up and down with wins and losses. We couldn't gain any real momentum, and because of that, Coach Porter was forced to retire. I understand now that our budget never really allowed us to operate the way we needed for consistent success. Regardless, Coach Porter gave me the opportunity of a lifetime, and I'll never forget the impact he made on my life.

My experiences in college changed my entire outlook on the world, life, and my purpose. I left Central State with lifelong friends. Aaron "Tron" Williams along with other teammates became my brothers for life. I had exceptional teammates and coaches on and off the court that each brought out the competitor in me. I was not a great player, but I was a phenomenal leader.

And throughout my life, I always had the ability to lead others. Identifying this ability while I was in college helped shape my career.

Four years previously, I drove away from the poverty, drugs, and crime that riddled Detroit in my white Mustang, full of hope and big dreams. And then, there I sat in a cap and gown surrounded by classmates, professors, friends, and family. When I looked to my left, I saw all of my teammates and coaches standing tall and proud. When I looked to the right, I saw all the people that I called my family who had each helped me in various ways.

And when I looked forward, far beyond the podium and stage, all I saw was possibility. Possibility for a future that many people thought I'd never reach. Possibility that so many in my neighborhood never got the opportunity to imagine; possibility that came to me when I never thought it would, and a responsibility to prove that anyone can accomplish anything if they stay committed. I smiled at Marlene as our eyes met across the room, hoping that she felt all of the love and gratitude I had for everything she'd ever done for me. And when my name was finally called, I sat there for just a moment to fully inhale the claps and cheering I heard in the background. I stood with my head held high and walked onto the stage. I looked out into the audience at the beautiful life God had laid out for me, and just at that very instant, at that specific moment in time, I saw my mother's face smiling back at me. It was in this single moment that I realized I made her dreams come true. On June 15, 1996, I was the first person in my entire family to graduate from college.

Through all the challenges I overcame in my life, it still amazes me how far I've come. That evening, Aunt Gloria, Le Le, Woo, Ray, and the entire Foster family celebrated me at a dinner. I didn't know I was supposed to give a speech that evening, so I did a terrible job with that, but it will always be one of the most memorable days of my life. All I could do was thank God. Without His guidance, none of this was possible.

Upon graduation, I was blessed with two unbelievable opportunities. When the new basketball coach, Michael Grant, was hired at CSU, he offered me a position the following year as a graduate assistant. Meaning, I would be working within the basketball program, and pursuing a master's degree. It was already huge for me to graduate with an undergraduate degree; getting a master's degree superseded that goal. In college basketball, becoming a grad assistant is usually one of the first steps someone takes en route to becoming a coach.

The second offer I received was from Oronde for a position as the Junior Varsity Coach Head Coach and Assistant Varsity Coach at Central High School back in Detroit.

Marlene was still living in Dayton, and because I was familiar with the CSU program, I was leaning toward staying at CSU and becoming a graduate assistant. Lance, my kinsman and roommate at the time, was moving back to Detroit, so I figured this would be a perfect time for Marlene and me to move in together. I could continue to help the Marauder program grow, and also get a master's degree. But as much as I wanted to stay to be with Marlene, I knew I had to consider the bigger picture.

> I made a decision to embark on a career that I felt resonated in my heart, which I now understand was key to how far I was able to come. If you think about it, how can you commit 100% of yourself to something that doesn't move you personally? The answer to that is, you can't. But once you find the path that is true to who you are, it will lead you throughout your career. It is very important to have the patience and courage to stay on your journey.

I was torn between the two offers. After thinking long and hard, the time came for me to make a final decision. My high school coach's voice crept back into my head, "You need to graduate from college with a degree in education, and come back to Detroit to coach." He was right. The opportunity to take over a program with Oronde was too good to pass up. My gut told me to move back home and take on the challenge. So, I did.

Chapter Five

ON THE BRINK

It was a quiet, sunny summer afternoon in August when Lance and I packed up the U-Haul. We would both be leaving so many amazing memories behind us as we moved back to Detroit. Just like any other time in my life when a major change was happening, I had a heavy heart full of emotion paired with the knowledge that I was making the right decision. A new chapter of my life and career was on the horizon.

We spent the entire day preparing for our departure and ended up staying one more night before getting on the road. That night, I thought about everything that had happened so far in my life, and I was thankful. Marlene crept into my mind as I daydreamed about the future. I thought that maybe one day when I was settled into my own place and steady in my career, we could really do it. I could marry her and live in a house and have children, you know… do it all the right way. I knew that these next steps could open the door for that possibility.

The night before I left, when I saw Marlene, we promised to really make an effort to sustain our relationship, even with the distance set between us. If we couldn't overcome a three-hour drive, then we weren't meant to be together. But no matter how hard I tried, that overwhelming feeling of change took over. Nothing would ever be exactly the same. I left Ohio a different person than I when I arrived. The growth I underwent gave me a completely different outlook, and I could feel in my bones that I was on the brink of something special.

Once we arrived in Detroit, we headed straight to Tracey Street. My aunt and uncle were happy to let me move back into their basement for the time being. My brother Woo, cousin Torin, and long-time neighbors were all awaiting my arrival. Everyone around me was so excited and proud of what I accomplished. To many people in the neighborhood, I had made it. In their eyes, leaving Detroit to play college basketball and returning a graduate was a big deal. But for me, it just added more pressure. I had to keep going. I had to keep defying the odds. I HAD to keep reaching higher.

When the school year started, I officially secured my first job coaching job at Central High School. I wasn't really familiar with the school, besides the fact that it was home to legendary songstress Anita Baker, and that they had a great football coach, Woody Thomas. Out of curiosity, I asked Oronde that day what made him choose me. He responded with, "It's my first head coaching job, and I need someone who I know and trust, who's ready to grind and take building a state championship program seriously. Along with that, not many of us go away to school and handle business like you did. I'm proud of you for doing that because I know where you come from. I know how hard that was."

His words meant a lot to me and I never forgot them. I went into the season with a beast mode mentality. I was determined not to let him down. As a high school coach, I would still need to get a better paying job because the coaching salary was only $3,500 per year. The following week, I went over to the Detroit School Center Building to apply for a teaching position. I was aware that there was a shortage of African-American male teachers in Detroit, so landing a spot would be easy for me. They told me I'd likely get a call that same day, and they were right. Within the next seventy-two hours, I had twelve offers. My degree was specific to Elementary Education; therefore, I had to start at that level before I could teach any upper level grades. I chose to work at the Detroit Performing Arts Academy because the principal and I had a great phone interview. Our conversation was different from all of the others, which is the major reason I felt it was the place for me. I accepted her offer a few days later to teach a fifth grade Language Arts class.

On the first day of school, the parents greeted me with such excitement because I would be their children's teacher for the year. I was young with a ball of energy as I greeted everyone in our building and throughout the community. The entire community was very supportive with the path of my life which prompted strangers in the neighborhood to become familiar with who I was. All the well wishes made me feel I made the right decision, though my journey from student to teacher wasn't without some hiccups.

I quickly noticed that I missed the "decorate your classroom memo" that every other teacher abided by on the first day. Every wall in my classroom was completely bare. That evening, I went to The Teacher's Store and got a few things to brighten up the place. All of the young teachers were paired with more experienced teachers for the first few weeks to develop their individual techniques. For some strange reason, students naturally had a respect for me. When I spoke, everyone in the room completely stopped talking. I commanded all eyes and ears without much resistance.

By the second week of school, we held our first open gym for the team at Central High and potential newcomers. It was a Tuesday afternoon when Oronde introduced me to the players we would be working with that season. There was a decent amount of talent on the team, but for some reason they had trouble winning the previous year. The first day, we just observed and I instantly saw the talent Oronde mentioned. Dante Darling, Jermaine Gambrail, Pierre Brooks, Chris Bailey, Jimmy Tyman, and a few others really showed out that day. As practice came to an end, Oronde leaned over to me and said, "Two of the best players that will be starters are not even in here today." He was referring to junior forward, Antonio Gates, and senior guard, Dwight Smith, who were both still in season with the varsity football team.

Dwight was the fastest 100-meter runner in the state, and Antonio was known to dominate in just about every sport. The next day, Oronde arranged open gym again, but this time we actually played with the guys. Obviously, we were both still in great shape, but the young guys gave us a run for our money. It was fun getting to know our team and making the transition from player to coach.

The following Friday, we went up to Joe Dumars Fieldhouse to participate in the fall league they were having. Oronde had me coach the team to gain some experience before our first game. Getting a taste of leading the players and calling plays was exhilarating. I was hooked on coaching.

Antonio came to Joe Dumars to play with us as well, even though he was still in football season. And after seeing these guys play against the other competition, I knew we could be special. I just couldn't figure out why they didn't win the previous year. These guys were so talented! Initially, I thought Dante Darling was the best player in our program. He stood 6'6", played left-handed, and was a DOG. He could score on the block, had a decent handle, was an adequate passer, and a GREAT rebounder! Antonio was a little chubby and unassuming, but did have skills and quick feet. I continued to preach to everyone that Dante was our best player after watching the team the first three weeks. Once football season came to an end, Antonio and his basketball game fully arrived.

Antonio showed me pretty quickly why everyone in the city knew how talented he was. Without seeing any other high school teams, I was confident that no one in the city was more talented than us. The only major challenge we really had was a mental one. How could we get sixteen and seventeen year olds to buy into the program we were trying to put in place given the fact that we were two new young coaches? Oronde and I were only twenty-three and twenty-two years old at the time. However, as I look back, being able to relate to the students was the key. We were all listening to the same music, and interested in the same pop culture. None of my previous coaches listened to 2Pac, Biggie Smalls and Jay Z. Being able to share these commonalities brought our players close to us very quickly. It was extremely helpful that the players took to us and were eager to listen and learn.

Eventually, we had to attend the Public School League (PSL) coaching meetings. I was in awe when I walked into our first meeting at Calihan Hall. All the coaches we sat amongst were coaches we competed against as high school players a few years ago. It was unbelievable that we were about to be on the sidelines coaching against Harry Harriston, Ben Kelso, Robert Menefee, and Johny Golston. When we walked out of that first meeting, Coach Harriston pulled Oronde and I to the side and said, "Listen young bucks, it's gonna be tough for you young guys. Take your ass whoppings and be patient. It's nothing personal, but you gotta learn to take ass whoppings early in your careers and y'all will be all right."

Neither of us said a word. Oronde chuckled, but we would never forget that statement, especially since Coach Harriston's Northern team would be opening the season against us at Central HS.

We continued to bond, teach, and get all of our guys to understand the big picture. They had never won at a high level, and neither had we as coaches. But we were determined to build something special. As the pre-season was coming to an end, my beloved Mazda 626 was no longer holding up. It also didn't suit my lifestyle anymore. As a coach, I had players in and out of my car all the time. I even took a few of them home regularly after practice. I decided it was time to get my first SUV, a green Ford Explorer. It was perfect for driving around several players.

It was December 5th, and our season opener had finally arrived. We had on our home white uniforms, and were laced in our black Iverson's. This Reebok shoe deal was the first basketball shoe deal ever at Central HS. I was dapper on the sideline in my Coogi sweater, black slacks, and alligator shoes. Northern High had Lamar Bigsby and Tyson Retney with a good supporting line up, along with Hall of Fame Coach Harriston. They were picked to win the game by a huge margin, so they walked on the floor with supreme confidence. It was a great game the first half, but we totally dominated them in the second half, and won the game by eighteen points. We ended up handing Coach Harriston the ass whooping, and boy did it feel good!

This signaled the beginning of the end for the older regime of coaches in the PSL. Folks around the city believed our win was a fluke, but we continued to dominate our competition, and beat Northern AGAIN on their court a month later. We ended up making the city playoffs for the first time in twenty years! However, we lost in the semifinals to Redford High School, coached by defensive guru, Derrick McDowell. After that loss, we began to focus on winning the state title. After a successful regular season, we knew it was a possibility we could make a run to win the Class A state championship, a feat that had not been accomplished at Central HS in a long time. Our success and growth throughout the season gave us all the belief that would win it all!

Popcorn at the Breslin Center (Michigan State's home court) never smelled so good! The atmosphere was so thick you could cut the tension with a knife! After four state playoff victories we were in the Final 4, and ready to take on Redford HS again. With revenge on the mind, we were prepared and ready! Back and forth we rumbled but the Huskies would prevail. Jason Predator and Omar Zeigler made great plays down the stretch to will their team to victory. We had a great season and our championship foundation was laid! The immediate future was bright in Trailblazer country!

When the season came to a close, we started working on things we knew we needed to improve to win next year. We also had to start thinking about how we would replace our best players, Dante and Antonio, who were approaching their senior year. This is when I would start to understand the art and importance of recruiting. If we wanted to be successful coaches, we needed to take a page out the book of the fabled coach, Perry Watson. Recruit, recruit, and recruit some more. It is the only way you could win consistently.

As July approached, Oronde and I decided to become roommates. He was living in Detroit, and I was looking to move out of my aunt's house. We added a third roommate, Duran Watkins. "D Watt" was Oronde's teammate at Wayne State. The boy had a deadly jump shot with the voice of Luther Vandross. After we settled into our new place, some of our players would stop by occasionally, but nobody more than Antonio. He loved playing John Madden Football. We spent the entire summer playing video games all day and all night. Our staff and players had such a great camaraderie. Everyone shared the same common goal and that was to win the Class A state championship the following season.

It was April 1997, and I hopped on the highway in a rush to spring workouts, and as soon as I turned up the radio, sirens came rolling in from behind a few minutes later. The police were signaling me to pull over, and I didn't understand why. I may have been driving a little over the speed limit, but there was no way I was going fast enough to be pulled over. When the officer came to my window he said, "Hey, Rob, can I see your license, registration, and insurance?"

Suddenly, an unmarked police car pulled in front of me, and another gentleman without a police uniform approached my passenger's side window and said, "Hey, Rob, how are you?"

"Good, but I'm trying to figure out why I was pulled over, and how everyone knows my name?" I replied.

"We know a lot more than your name. We know you live on Scotia, you're a teacher at Detroit Performing Art Academy, and you visit an apartment in Southfield quite often. What's your relationship with Deon Griffin? Before you answer that, I want you to know I'm FBI Agent Moscatio, and we've been watching you for a while now. As you know, Deon is in our custody, and we would like to interview you at our downtown office within the next seventy-two hours. Take my card. If we don't hear from you in the next twenty-four hours with a scheduled time, we'll be coming to get you ourselves. Have a goodnight, and don't worry about the speeding ticket," the agent said.

When I pulled off, my heart was beating out of control. I knew the FBI had raided all of Deon's properties a few weeks earlier, arrested him, and were holding him until his court date. But what did that have to do with me? I had done nothing illegal. I questioned getting an attorney, but wondered if that would make it look like I was hiding something. I decided to call the number on the card a few hours later to set up the appointment. The next day, I drove downtown, and my heart was racing yet again. Were they planning to throw me into something I wasn't a part of to get information they assumed I knew? I had one option, and that was to tell the truth so I could move on.

I sat in an interrogation room with three agents, and the grilling began. Question after question after question, then repeats of the same questions. Fortunately for me, and only by the grace of God, I could not identify a single person in the pictures they put in front of me. I didn't know one of the names they inquired about, and I never visited California where the transactions were happening. After ninety minutes of no help towards the investigation, they let me go. When I walked out, the agent said he'd be in touch again within the next thirty days, but I never heard from him again. A few months later Deon was sentenced to eight to fifteen years in prison for conspiracy to deliver drugs and money laundering. Wow, just think about it… If I would have made one wrong turn and stayed involved with Deon and the drug game back in high school, I could have easily been in the exact same situation, serving time in prison. Moments like that one kept me focused and determined.

In hindsight, and even though I was telling the truth, I should have asked for a lawyer. Parents, mentors, guardians – have this discussion with young people you love. I was fortunate, the officers I was being interrogated by were after the truth, and I found out that they had been following me for quite some time. They respected what I was trying to do with my life, as a teacher and a coach. Additionally, it is important to note that my background had allowed me to handle the pressure of the questioning. It is just smart for anyone to be represented by an attorney at a time like this. My situation turned out fine, but not all people are equipped to withstand this type of environment.

By the time the beginning of the school year approached, our guys had competed in several Amateur Athletic Union (AAU) tournaments, including the nationally known Adidas Big Time Tournament that is held in Las Vegas every July. Mentally and physically, everyone was confident and ready for the upcoming season.

After being in a long-distance relationship for a year, things started to take a toll on my relationship with Marlene. We tried our best to make it work, but I was growing in a different direction, while putting all of my time and focus on my career. The weekend visits started to slow down because something basketball related always took priority. It became too hard to maintain the relationship. My career took the forefront of my thoughts and so much had transpired since I moved backed to Detroit.

One Sunday that September, my friends demanded that I go out with them. We all met up for Soul Night at the State Theater. Soul Night was the biggest party in Detroit. It was mainly an event for street guys and women looking for men who had street money. I was dressed in beige slacks, a cream shirt, and peach-colored alligator shoes. As I walked in, I couldn't help but notice this one sexy woman who wouldn't stop staring at me. I started to think maybe there was something on my face because she continuously whispered to her friend as she stared. When we got a little closer to where she was standing, she spoke to me.

"Hey, what's your name?

"Rob," I replied.

"What do you do for a living?" she asked.

Sheesh, this girl was forward, I thought to myself.

"What do YOU do for a living?" I flipped back onto her.

"No, that's what I asked you! Now, what do you do?" she asked again.

"I'm a school teacher. I came down here with some friends, but this really isn't my kinda party. I don't really go out much," I explained.

"Good, my name is Shun, give me your number right quick."

I quickly gave her my number, and she walked away. I didn't see her for the rest of the night. To my surprise, the next morning Shun called and we had a really good conversation. We started to develop a friendship that would eventually turn into a relationship within the next few months. Shun and I had a lot in common. We were the same age, college graduates, and both had goals to become successful in the education field. Shun was an only child who was very spoiled and could only see things her way. After a year of dating, I realized that no matter how much I loved someone, if they didn't like or understand the commitment it took for a coach to become successful, the relationship could not work. With all the good Shun brought to the table, she never understood the sacrifices I had to make, but I continued to give it a try.

Before the school year began, I received a call from my childhood school, Bagley Elementary. I was told their Physical Education teacher was retiring, and was asked if I was interested in the position. Of course, I was! What are the odds that I would get an opportunity to teach at the elementary school that took me in when I was denied by every other elementary school in the city? I jumped at the chance. Bagley was also closer to Central High, making it easier for me to travel to practice and games. On the first day of school, I got reacquainted with some of the very same teachers that taught me when I was a student. Once I settled in, it was a great feeling to be teaching at a school that I could call home.

We continued to work extremely hard as we went into our second season at Central High, and finished with a record of eighteen wins and two losses. One of those losses was to Clarkson HS that had "Mr. Basketball," Dan Fife. During that particular game, Antonio vomited in the middle of the court from being out of shape, and eating too much before tipoff. The other loss was to an average Northwestern team led by Wadell Henry. They played great, and we played worse than we ever had. It was just one of those strange days. We ended up losing in the semifinals of the city playoffs against a good Cass Tech team led by PG Marlon Williamson. They hit some incredible shots in overtime and beat us that day. That was one of the worse losses we endured in our first two seasons.

After losing to Cass Tech, we all knew there was only one more championship left, and that was for the state title. Central High had not won a state title in eighty-two years. We had a team full of talented seniors, and we made them understand how special it would be if we could pull off this great feat. Plus, we were close to winning the title the year before. Our experience would be helpful, but the key would be to get everyone to sacrifice their personal goals for the team's goals. This was our last opportunity to do so. We had all the pieces; we just needed to put them into action. We played against my alma mater, Mumford High school, in the first game, and then defeated a very talented Pershing High School team, coached by the great Johnny Golston, in the district finals. It was a very close game.

After winning the following two games, we were set to face Dan Fife and the Clarkson team that had beat us earlier in the season. This was the quarterfinal game that would take us back to the Final Four at the Breslin Center. Ferndale gym was packed to capacity with standing room only available. The first half was back and forth with consistent lead changes. During the third quarter, Clarkson took a twelve-point lead, and there was definitely concern on the faces throughout the crowd. Dante and Antonio argued as we called, "Timeout!" Dante felt Antonio was trying to make it a one-on-one game versus Fife, and wasn't passing the ball to his teammates. He was so furious in the huddle; no one could calm him down.

I remember stepping in, addressing Dante, and trying to remind him of the big picture. Antonio and everyone else were quiet the entire time. Antonio looked at Dante and just shook his head. Antonio was never the one to get caught up in one-on-one battles, so he remained focused on the play. As Oronde observed Dante's energy, he decided the next two plays would be for him. When we left that timeout we saw, "Dante, half hook on the right block, GOOD. Antonio drive and drop to Dante, DUNK. Dante elbow jump shot, GOOD!" and as Dante back pedaled down the court, he finally cracked a smile as we were on a 6-0 run and back in our groove. We forced Clarkson to call a time out. We finished the third quarter with a flurry, and played very well in the fourth to close Clarkson out.

Just like that, we punched our ticket to the Final Four! We breezed through our semifinal game, which put us in the championship game versus Belleville. There would be NO denying the Central High Trailblazers now. We beat Belleville 63-47 in the state championship game. I remember hugging Oronde with tears of joy as the clock struck zero. It was such an emotional feeling to bring a state championship back to Central High. That day we made history!

One of the reasons winning it all meant even more to me was the fact that the late Dott Wilson was on our coaching staff. Dott was a former head coach at Central High who invested forty years of his life in the program, and later played a major role at Detroit's famed St. Cecilia's gym, known affectionately as the Saint. Dott bled blue and white, so we were all very happy that Dott, Mr. Central himself, was part of our new regime, and helped us win the title. That year, Dott called Oronde "Mr. Lucky" because he could not believe what we as coaches were already accomplishing in our mid-twenties, after only two years.

When I walk into the gymnasium at Central High today, I get goose bumps. There is still a banner hanging with all of our names embroidered on it. It is a nice reminder of what we accomplished, one of the greatest days of my career. After we won the state title, I was approached with several job openings, and though I was grateful for the opportunity Oronde had given me, I was ready to branch off on my own.

Chapter Six

THREE YEARS TO ROCKETT

The summer after winning the state championship at Central High, I interviewed for five different head coaching positions in Detroit. Those interviews were with Renaissance, Northwestern, Henry Ford, Cooley, and Crockett high schools. Truth be told, absolutely no one wanted the position at Crockett. The facilities at Crockett were beyond terrible. Their classes were held in trailers, and they didn't have a gym. It was no surprise that Crockett was known to have the worst sports program in the whole city. The school consisted of maybe a handful of true athletes. In fact, the previous year we beat Crockett at Central High by a whopping sixty points.

As fate, or rather bad luck would have it, I ended up being turned down by every school I interviewed with except Crockett! With only one job opportunity in hand, I considered returning to Central High another year and waiting on a better opportunity to come along. But after discussing it with Oronde, he advised me to take the opportunity if I ever wanted to be a varsity head coach. I just needed to understand that I was walking into a completely different situation than what we had at Central High. My other close friend, Murray, was on his way to be the coach at Southeastern High School, and told me to take the job so we could all be head coaches.

"How incredible would it be for each of us to accomplish this right around the same time?" Murray wondered out loud.

He was right. After thinking about it for a few weeks and dodging calls from the school's athletic director, Doris Rodgers, I decided to go for it.

"Give me three years, and I'm gonna win a state championship at Crockett. Remember me saying this guys, and if I don't, I'm done there. I'm gonna give myself three years." As we stood in Murray's drive way on Monte Vista St.

Oronde and Murray both looked at me and chuckled. I called Mrs. Rogers the following morning and accepted the job.

My first year at Crockett was tedious to say the least. I started the season with zero players who actually LOVED the game of basketball. Everyone who was already on the team at Crockett was doing it purely for recreational purposes. For the first four months, I regretted taking on what felt like an impossible task. Verynda McClain, a math teacher and the cheerleading coach at Crockett, became a very close friend of mine during this difficult time. Because Verynda was a graduate of Michigan University and loved sports, she really understood high-level athletics, and was the only person at Crockett who could relate to my frustrations. After sulking through my entire first year, I realized I had no choice but to make it work and be "all in" as I love to reference. The first season we won a total of four out of eighteen games. I knew we were improving from the previous year, but I never experienced this much losing ever in my life. Nothing bothers me more than losing. My time at Crockett showed me this.

On the other hand, the Crockett administration was grateful that we only lost fourteen games. I was actually praised for this nonsense! "You're doing a tremendous job, coach," said Mrs. Betty Berry (assistant principal) after every game, but I couldn't see it. I was determined not to settle for mediocrity.

> If you are not "all in," then you don't really want it bad enough. This applies to school, work, your love life, and everything you do. Passion without commitment will only get you but so far. I didn't realize this at the time, but it's important to understand that you will lose in life more often than you win. Therefore, there's no need to be afraid of failure. Failure should never deter you from chasing success.

When the first season ended, I put my recruiting hat on. Crockett would definitely be hard to sell, but I had no choice but to really go for it if I was going to reach the level of success I'd hoped to within three years. My good friend, Greg Martin, allowed us to use the Tindal recreation center to practice throughout the summer and into my second season. I was at Tindal so much, I decided to get a job there for the summer. What better place to be while trying to recruit kids, practice and make some extra money?

Rico Benson, a co-worker at the recreation center, told me about his little cousin who was trying to leave Southfield HS for a better opportunity. I was interested in any and every player who would even "think" about attending Crockett. Rico's cousin was named Maurice Ager. A few days later, he brought Maurice up to Tindal to meet me. Maurice happened to have a broken wrist at this time, so I wasn't able to actually watch him play. Instead we talked, and about twenty minutes later, Maurice was sold on coming to play for me! His best friend, Phil Jones, who came along with him to the gym, ended up being sold on coming to Crockett as well. Now, I just needed to convince their parents to allow them to actually leave Southfield and attend Crockett, which was not in close proximity. Both families initially told me it probably wouldn't work because they had no way to get them to and from the school. I thought about their transportation concerns, and then circled back with an offer on the table.

"If I pick the boys up for school and bring them home every day after practice, could they come to Crockett?"

Maurice's mom didn't believe I was actually willing to drive almost an hour each way to take Mo to and from practice, but I was determined to have him on the team.

"You have my word on this. I promise! I live in Southfield, so I can grab them as I'm on my way to work."

Ms. Ager finally gave in and allowed Maurice to attend. Soon after, Phil's grandmother was also on board. This was my first-ever recruiting class, which turned out to be one of the most important classes of my career. With the addition of Mo and Phil, combined with captain Dre Johnson, Yared Yearby, and Rob Richardson, Crockett basketball was ready to take off. The next three years I never missed a day of work. My commitment went beyond basketball. I knew if I was late or missed work Mo and Phil (later came Dwight Collins) would miss class which is inexcusable! I won the perfect attendance award every year I worked at Crockett HS.

That fall was super exciting for us. To have upgraded talent along with a new assistant coach, LaBaron German, Crockett was on the rise. Coach German is the best shooting coach I've ever worked with, "put your hand in the cookie jar... hold it" was the consistent phrase during all shooting drills and individual workouts. We practiced at several different recreation centers because we still didn't have our own gym. And despite these challenges, we won sixteen regular season games. The buzz around the city was that Crockett was no longer the underdog. We went on to win the school's FIRST EVER district championship. We were eliminated the following game by Renaissance

HS, who was led by All-American, Ricky Paulding. After that loss, I reiterated to my team that we were on the verge of doing something extraordinary.

It wasn't long before Mo emerged as one of the top players in the state. His determination to be the best was second to none. I was confident if we could somehow keep this group together the entire summer, we would have the opportunity to win the state championship the following season. The summer would be an important time for improvement and developing team chemistry. We held individual workouts at Tindal while attending several summer team camps. Our best camp experience was the Bob Huggins overnight camp at the University of Cincinnati. We ended up winning the championship, which was a great sign for what would come. Over the summer our captain, Andre Johnson, became a great leader. Dre began to take on my personality as a player which helped his success and the overall confidence of our team.

During this time, the AAU basketball scene began to heat up as the stakes were high – and have continued to grow in this area of basketball. The most relevant AAU teams in the state of Michigan were the Mustangs (Adidas grassroots) and the Family (Nike grassroots). The Mustangs had the state's best players, coached by Norm Oden and Chris Grier. Grier was positioning himself to take over the Mustang program after doing a tremendous job of bringing national notoriety to the program. The leaders of the Family, Speedy Walker and Vince Baldwin, did not care much for Grier. They felt that Grier was too aggressive when recruiting, and he had a "by any means necessary" attitude about landing players. If they were the best, he was determined to get them in a Mustangs' uniform.

In early November, everyone in the basketball world of Michigan was at Crisler Arena to watch the University of Detroit play Michigan. Rashad Phillips (#2319), who is one of the most underrated and best players to ever come out of the state of Michigan, dropped 30 points and had 9 assists in a game Michigan ultimately won, but halfway through the 2nd half the real show got started.

Out of nowhere, we could all hear Tim Ferguson, the best promoter in all of basketball, who decided to channel Don King. Ferg yelled, "Vince, Grier bitch ass is right behind us." Vince bought in quickly, turned to Grier who is one row behind, and says, "I should slap you." Everyone was sitting in suspense and could not believe this was actually happening inside Crisler Arena. Grier replied, "Try me if you want." While sitting in rows 5 and 6 at mid-court, they both stood up, clinched their fists and squared off. After exchanging, "what's up" about 20 times, Vince finally took the first swing and haymakers followed after that. Security rushed over to break it up and escorted both guys out of the arena.

I could not believe that the competition of AAU basketball had grown men acting out Thrilla in Manila, at a Michigan basketball game in front of 13,000 fans, coaches, and recruits while representing the two major shoe companies. The following year, Grier decided to make a power move. With the blessing of Sonny Vacarro, he started his own AAU program.

> The uncertainty surrounding college basketball is exemplified by the FBI investigations currently going on in the NCAA. The competitive nature around basketball was and always will be fierce… with everyone involved starving for money and success.

Shun and I had now been in a committed relationship for three years. But she still lacked the understanding necessary for her to date a coach, and had no interest in basketball. Every day Shun nagged me, "Why are you at practice so late? Why do you have to always drop kids off at home? Why do you care about them more than you care about me?" I was constantly pushing her to see the big picture and my plan. I told her that if she just continued to focus on her career as an aspiring day care owner, and allowed me to grow as a coach, we would be a power couple one day. I begged her to trust me and stick with it, but she never stopped complaining. Meanwhile, Oronde and Murray were in the background with the same perspective.

"Murph, if you really wanna win the state championship this upcoming season, you need to let Shun go man. I'm telling you, she's not good for you at this time in your career! She's hindering your progress," said Murray.

It was hard to hear, but I knew it was the truth. I went into deep thought about the conversation, and I promised myself that the next time Shun threatened to break up, I would really let go and move forward. Exactly forty-eight hours later, we had an argument about something minor and she said it, "I need a break from this relationship!" I kindly replied, "Ok, I'll give you that." Several days passed and I refused to reach out to her, which wasn't the way things normally went. So, she starting calling me, confused as to why I wasn't chasing her the way I usually did. At this point, my mind was made up. I was moving on to focus on the season ahead. Nothing would make me go back to dating her again. I knew what was important, and what I needed became very clear for me. Shun was unable to see the big picture and because of that I had to let the situation go.

> To be successful, you need to be as efficient as you can possibly be. That means that you have to pay attention to where your energy is going. If there's something that brings you stress on a regular basis, you need to let it go to operate at your optimal level. This is important in all stages of life, but even more crucial early on when laying the groundwork for your career.

After an emotional summer of getting transfer commitments then de-commitments from Brandon Jenkins, Walter Waters and Terrance Price year three at Crockett was here! Spain Middle School, which was right next door to Crockett, agreed to let us use their gym as our home court. For the first time, Crockett basketball had a place to call home. Although Spain's court was not regulation sized, it was an unforgettable experience to play in the "Hot Box." We dominated our competition throughout the regular season, finishing 16-1 going into the city playoffs. We won our first ever playoff game with ease against Murray Wright HS. The following game was against Redford HS, and they won by just a few points in the end. I was very proud of my team's performance, as Redford was the best team in the state. The following week, we played the consolation game versus Finney HS, and we lost again. My team was shocked when I broke down in tears in the locker room from losing two games in a row. The state tournament would begin the following week, and my reaction to our previous losses sent a specific message to the team. I was determined to win; this was not just a job for me. I believed we were talented and tough enough to win the Class B State Championship, and I refused to allow this opportunity to slip away.

In the district final, we faced Central High School. Three years later, the tables had turned. Oronde was coaching at Kent State University, and Central HS was not quite the same. After beating them in the district final, we knew there was no time to celebrate. The two-time, Class B back-to-back state champs, Orchard Lake St. Mary's, were waiting for us. They were a very well coached team with talented players. Charles Davis and Grant Mason were experienced champions and ready to defend their back to back crown. Davis gave us hell for three quarters. Rob Richardson would finally wake up. Yared Yearby and Dre Johnson were steady all night, and with Mo Ager's fourth quarter explosion, we were able to defeat the defending state champs by one point, 40-39!

The next week, we regrouped for regionals. Willow Run HS gave us nothing we couldn't handle. Punching our ticket to the Final Four that evening was UNBELIEVABLE! I was heading back to the Breslin Center with no Antonio Gates or Dante Darling. I had to RECRUIT my best players. I coached my team the best that I could without a gym, teaching inside a trailer, and with the threat of Crockett permanently closing. Yet through all of the negativity, my troops and I were accomplishing the unthinkable. I couldn't have been more proud, but knew that we weren't finished yet.

In our final moment of preparation, I emphasized detail and defense. I also talked about the discipline we needed on offense because I knew how the games would be called by the officials during the Final Four. Every time we touched our opponent, I anticipated a foul being called to put us in early foul trouble. My team needed to understand we could not beat ourselves by making bad decisions, taking bad shots, and not playing together. I wanted to make sure we were prepared for this opportunity on all levels!

The semifinal was a very low scoring game, and we were also in foul trouble. I decided to run our wide flex offense without taking a shot for the first four minutes of the fourth quarter while protecting a five-point lead. That night, our plan was executed to perfection. We won 53-44 versus Richland Lake Gull, and we were set to compete for the state championship the following day. Rest was imperative for such a quick turnaround, so we got our guys back to the Kellogg hotel right after the game. Film and scouting reports were essential because we would not be able to walk-through Coopersville's action with such a quick turn-around. After our team dinner and meeting my staff and I felt we did everything under our control to prepare our team to bring the state championship trophy back to Crockett high school.

The day of the state championship, you could cut the tension with a knife when you walked into the arena. I felt the same feelings and emotions I experienced three years earlier in that same locker room. As we took the floor of a sold out Breslin Center, 80% of the crowd was Coppersville fans. I remember getting off to a very sluggish start. The moment and the energy were at a heightened intensity that my team had never felt before. All of the players were trying to take the game into their own hands, and it wasn't long before we were down by ten points. Turnover after turnover along with bad shots forced me to call two timeouts to calm our guys down, but I knew we needed to get to halftime. I had stored up a tremendous amount of energy throughout the playoffs, and it was the perfect time to go "Izzoish" on my team! I shouted and challenged every one of our guys to play tougher and with more heart. We were playing out of character, and I needed everyone to focus on playing their role.

Three minutes into the third quarter, I decided to have a chat with the referee.

"Whitfield, do you see what these guys are doing?" I yelled.

"Calm down, Coach, most of the time, the calls break even," he said.

Wallace Whitfield was a black official working alongside two white officials who were calling a very lopsided game in favor of Coopersville. I felt my team was purposely being cheated out of a great opportunity. I continued to complain, so Whitfield told me to get my guys off the perimeter. He noted that maybe we should try driving the ball. That was the best coaching advice I received all game. From that point forward, the calls were clear.

We approached the next thirteen minutes with a new game plan. Our red defensive press ignited some turnovers led by our sixth man, Wallace Richards. We made a couple of easy buckets, and we were feeling good as we closed in on Coopersville to take the lead. Jumper by Dre, layup by Yearby, defensive charge taken by Richardson, explosive dunk by Mo Ager, GAME OVER! 49-40 was the final score, and Crockett HS was the NEW Class B State Champs!

Everyone at Crockett deserved a piece of the net! We were like the "little engine that could" that no one believed in. Tears rolled down my face uncontrollably. I could not stop crying! The game was televised on Fox Sports Detroit, and viewed by many. I received text messages and voicemails from several friends and coaches around the country that evening. I'm very thankful to referee Wallace Whitfield for calling a fair state championship game. My staff, LeBaron German, Robert Williams and Phil Garland did a tremendous job of helping me build Crokett into a championship program.

Right around the same time I won the championship, Bullet was back and staying with his sister, Aunt Gloria, on Tracey Street. Seeing him for the first time in years meant we had a lot to catch up on. Initially, I could tell something wasn't right about him, but I tried to ignore it. He still embodied his usual upbeat attitude that I knew and loved, but he didn't look like himself. My feelings were confirmed when I learned that Bullet had been recently diagnosed with lung cancer, and was in and out of the hospital going through chemo therapy. By March of that year, he was admitted to the hospital for good when the chemo was no longer working. It was a sunny day when Woo and I went to visit him that July. Bullet's vitals were down and he could barely communicate. His lack of responsiveness made us stick around that day instead of going back to work. Exactly one hour later, my brother and I watched Bullet take his last breath. We knew that this day was coming, but that didn't change how tragic the moment was. This experience was just as tough for me as it was for Woo. Even though he wasn't my biological father, he was as close as it would get. Aunt Gloria rushed to the hospital, and we all prayed over his body one last time.

Once we won the state championship, AAU season was right around the corner. For the past few years, I met with Nike and Adidas representatives because they were looking to sponsor programs and wanted their products worn by the best players possible at the grassroots level. That year, both Murray and I were approached with more deals than ever before. I won the state championship, and Maurice Ager became a household name. With the addition of Murray's players, Brandon Jenkins and Walter Waters we had our own "Big Three". However, I was most concerned with getting a deal in place for my next season at Crockett. Durand Walker and Vince Baldwin of the Family Organization AAU Program, who were already with Nike, suddenly had interest in getting the "big Three" to participate with their program. So, they decided to arrange a meeting with George Raveling, the president of Nike grassroots basketball, in downtown Detroit. The meeting was very productive. The only problem was that Nike's main priority was Mo Ager.

There was no interest in helping Crockett, and they knew they had time to hone in on Murray's players again next season.

Although I really wanted to sign with Nike, I didn't like how they treated me the previous year when I was in the early stages of building my program. The summer before we won the state title, I tried to get Mo into the Nike Jamboree All-American camp, but they ignored me. Things ended up just fine for Mo because he got some exposure playing for B-Real coached by Odis Bellinger who helped Mo grow in all areas of his life. Later that summer Mo also joined Team Detroit, which was headed by Rodney Heard, one of Detroit's most well-known basketball impresarios. Aside from running Team Detroit, Heard was a former college coach at University of California - Berkley who parlayed his experiences into stints with numerous NBA teams including the Memphis Grizzlies, Atlanta Hawks, New York Knicks and Milwaukee Bucks. Heard was one of a kind. Playing for Heard turned out to be a good thing at the time. Of course, now that we won the state championship a year later, everyone's tune had changed.

Adidas had a better deal on the table that would not only help Mo Ager, but Crockett HS as well. You would think that signing a deal with Adidas would have been a no-brainer, but as Jay-Z would say, the "Allure" of Nike was tough to overcome, so Murray and I decided to hold out. A month later when we were still undecided, an AAU coach approached Murray and I again in hopes of getting a deal done with us for his AAU program. We met one evening at a Friday's restaurant in Southfield, and after dinner, the coach slid us an envelope with $10,000 cash to make it happen. That was too much for two young guys to turn down. The deal was done. We walked out of there like we just became rich, and when we drove off, Murray was screaming and counting. We couldn't believe it! Young and dumb.

I could hardly sleep that night The novelty of us getting handed $10,000 in cash wore off, and something didn't sit well with me. I couldn't do it. I called Murray and told him we couldn't take the deal, and we needed to give back the money. Murray fought me on it but reluctantly came around. The next day, I drove over to Hampton Middle School where this coach's team was practicing and called it off.

Chris Grier, who was dissatisfied coaching the Michigan Mustangs AAU team, was waiting in the wings. Chris drove down from Flint to meet with Murray and I.

"Why don't you start your own program?" Murray and I asked Chris.

"You know what; I was thinking the same thing. I need to meet with Sonny Vacarro, the President of Adidas grassroots basketball, but I need the right players to do it," Chris said.

"Well, we have Mo Ager, Brandon Jenkins, Walt Walters and maybe Dion Harris – you have Anthony Roberson, Olu Famutimi and Matt Trannon. With these seven guys, who in the country would be better than us?" I said to Chris.

"I see where you're going, Murph."

We continued talking for hours every day until there was a deal in place, and the "Up In Smoke Tour" began! The team we started was called the Michigan Hurricanes, and we took the nation by storm. A few practices together and meetings at Daryl Greer's home, we were ready to blast off! Our first tournament was in Houston to play in the Adidas Classic, run by John Hurrie. This tournament put the program and Mo Ager on the map around the country. We played in the championship game versus a loaded Texas Bluechips team, coached by Mitch Malone. That team had Daniel Horton, Chris Bosh, and Ike Diogue to name a few. Though we fell short of a victory, Mo Ager dominated the game. Anthony Roberson, who was the state of Michigan's best player at the time, couldn't make the trip, so it was Mo's chance to show everyone what he was about, and he did just that! From there, we followed that tourney with a great trip to Bob Gibbon's event in North Carolina.

By the end of the spring, Mo Ager went from an unknown name to a Top 30 player in the country. He had turned into a hot commodity. Several schools were after Mo, but he only had a few offers on the table. The University of Detroit coached by Perry Watson was the first Division I school to offer him a scholarship. Then Marquette and Providence stepped in and were the first high-major schools to offer him scholarships. The University of Michigan and Michigan State had evaluated Mo several times, but didn't pull the trigger. However, when Tony Harvey and Mizzou arrived on the scene after Mo's breakout performance in Houston, the in-state powerhouses stepped up their recruitment of Mo. Coach Harvey changed the entire landscape of the recruitment. Mizzou flew into Detroit the following Monday to see Mo workout at the Tinal Recreation Center, then offered him a scholarship. Once Mizzou offered, Michigan State and the University of Michigan followed suit. From that point on, the race for Mo Ager was on. We narrowed it down to three schools: Missouri, Marquette, and Michigan State. Mizzou had a long-time presence in Detroit, recruiting players such as Arthur Johnson and Rick Paulding, who were currently playing with the Tigers. Mizzou's Coach Harvey, who was originally from Michigan, and Quin Snyder did a tremendous job making sure his presence was felt with Mo. Tom Crean and Dwayne Stephens were selling him on becoming Dwayne Wade's replacement at Marquette, and Tom Izzo was going to do everything he could to get Mo, especially after losing out on Anthony Roberson to Florida and Lester Abram to Michigan. A few weeks later Michigan's head coach, Tommy Amaker, decided to no longer recruit Mo to target Dion Harris who was on the next class. Coach Amaker and I continued to build a great relationship which lead to carte blanche inside his basketball program. I regularly attended Michigan basketball practices and games but nothing was more fun than spending time at Coach Amaker's home after games laughing (non-stop) as we (TA, Ra and Grier) watched the Kings of Comedy while sharing funny stories. I appreciate Coach Amaker for always welcoming me with open arms as I was learning more about the profession and life early in my coaching career. A class act!

There were several twists and turns throughout Mo's recruitment. This showed me how recruiting players was a cutthroat business. I was truly an amateur in the recruiting game, and this experience taught me a great deal. I believed that Mizzou or Marquette would have been the best choices for Mo to play early. The recruiting war began and it was non-stop from each school involved daily.

In the midst of all that was going on, I was given an opportunity to interview for a coaching position at Michigan State University, but didn't land the job. The fact that I was considered for a position at Michigan State was indicative of where my career was headed.

In July, the Michigan Hurricanes kept rolling, and my career got another huge boost as well. Mo got invited to compete in the prestigious ABCD Camp in New Jersey, and I got an opportunity to coach at the camp. While working at the camp, I formed relationships with coaches, players, and basketball power brokers that helped build my recruiting network. It was here at ABCD camp where I met Sonny Vaccaro, Chris Rivers, Gary Charles and the entire adidas staff. I had an opportunity to coach and/or watch Chris Bosh, Carmelo Anthony, LeBron James, Raymond Felton, Sean May, Sean Dockery, Lenny Cooke and other high-level basketball players. This was a tremendous experience that I continue to benefit from today.

The recruiting process began to wear on Mo and his family. After weighing his options with his family, Mo called Quin Snyder and committed to Missouri. Mo's next job was to be tough enough to make the calls to the few programs we felt he was letting down. Surprisingly after Mo spoke with Tom Crean and Tom Izzo, Mo called Quin Snyder back 48 hours later and de-committed from the Tigers. Then 24 hours later, WAM BAM JAM, Mo committed to Michigan State to play for Hall of Fame coach Tom Izzo. Essentially, it became a battle of two against one as Mo was making his final calls. Missouri couldn't outlast the bashing that came from those two good friends helping each other. Mo's decision to attend Michigan State turned out to be the best situation in the long run. The information told to Mo and his family during the close-out of the recruiting process was vicious. The words used to describe Missouri were so bad and insulting that when Tony Harvey ran into Tom Crean in Orlando a week later, there were expletives exchanged immediately. It became so heated that Crean's assistant, Dwayne Stephens grabbed Tony Harvey to break the two apart. Mo's recruitment definitely prepared me for my future recruiting battles.

As July was coming to a close the Hurricanes played in the Adidas Big Time Tournament in Las Vegas a few weeks later. It was one of the GREATEST summers of my life! I learned so much in such a short period of time. It was time to focus on defending our state title which was exciting.

After summer basketball ended, I was ready to put myself in the position to get an opportunity at the college level following the upcoming season. With all the relationships I made around the country, I knew anything was possible. Defending any championship is always a tough task. After a good regular season, we lost in the regional finals in a tough game to River Rouge HS on a tip-in shot by Lou Hamilton, just as time expired. I had a strong feeling this would be the last game I coached at Crockett.

On the bus ride home, all I could think about was my team giving up a tip-in as the horn sounded. I had no idea where I was going, but God was telling me this was it. After building this program into one of the most competitive programs in the state, I needed a new challenge. Once the season ended, we prepared for AAU basketball, and I attended some NCAA tournament games. In fact, this was the year I went to watch Kent State University, led by Antonio Gates and Oronde on the coaching staff, defeat Pittsburgh to advance to the Elite 8 in Lexington KY at Rupp Arena. It was during this trip that I met Kent State's assistant coach, Jim Christian, who would eventually give me my first opportunity to become an assistant coach at the Division I level.

If you want to be successful in this world you have to grind. You have to wake up each morning and be someone who is committed to whatever it is you're passionate about. Only then will you have a shot at success. I was 100% committed to do what people thought was impossible at Crockett HS. Giving anything less than 100% of yourself isn't truly a commitment. There is no way that I could have been 89% invested and achieved the same results. Once you figure out what you're truly passionate about, it will be easier to stay committed. There's no better feeling than having to go to work every day, and it not feel like work at all. When you accomplish that feeling, you will know real passion. I didn't have a master plan when I took the Crockett job. But I decided to grind my way through the obstacles. Always remember that success is built in your routine!

Chapter Seven

WHO BETTER THAN ROB MURPHY?

After Kent State lost in the Elite 8, Stan Heath, the head coach, accepted a more prestigious head coaching position at the University of Arkansas. The next in line to take Stan's position was either Oronde or Jim Christian, who were both assistant coaches for Kent State at the time. But because Oronde only had one year of college coaching experience, Kent State elected to go with Jim. When the time came for Jim to figure out who to hire for his support staff, Oronde recommended me for an assistant coach position because he was expecting to leave with Stan and go to Arkansas. When Jim consulted Stan on this decision, Stan agreed that I should be the man for the job. Not only would it benefit them to hire a good coach and recruiter from the Detroit area, but I was someone they believed could get senior forward Antonio Gates to continue performing at the highest level possible. Who better than Rob Murphy?

Before I could be offered the job at Kent State, Stan needed to secure a spot for Oronde with him at Arkansas. Otherwise, the assistant position wouldn't be open for me at Kent because Oronde would stay. The process hit a speed bump when Chris Grier-Luchey, who is a good friend of Stan's, started advising him NOT to hire Oronde. Chris wasn't sold on Oronde because Oronde was a Nike affiliate and they didn't see eye to eye. You have to remember that Chris, who partnered with me to form the Michigan Hurricanes, was linked to Adidas, Nike's bitter rival.

"Oronde will not be going to Arkansas! I don't care what he told you, I'm telling you, he ain't going nowhere!" Chris shouted.

Somehow, I needed to convince Chris to disregard the shoe company alliances and support Oronde for the position. I called Chris back the following day to explain that if Oronde didn't get the Arkansas spot, I wouldn't get the assistant position at Kent State. Reluctantly, Chris understood my perspective. And I'm thankful he did.

"Murph, I'm gonna do this for you, so you can become a college coach. But, Oronde better understand who helped him moving forward. Oronde tends to get amnesia all the time, and forgets who helps him. I don't wanna do this, but I'm gonna do this for you."

Chris stood by his word. Oronde was hired at Arkansas, and everything aligned for me. I was leaving high school basketball behind and accepted the offer as an assistant coach at Kent State University. I was excited and ready for this great opportunity. For years, I had worked to build relationships and learn from several college assistant coaches (Tony Harvey, Mick Cronin, Brian Gregory, Dwayne Stephens, Lamonte Stone, Phil Seymore, Stan Heath, David Greer, Curtis Townsend, and Dave Leitao) I was ready to take on this new challenge.

In my final days at Crockett, I spent all my time with my players. My seniors, Mo Ager, Phil Jones, and Ezekiel Adams had done so much for both the Crockett program and my career; I could not thank them enough. Without them and my former players, Dre Johnson, Rob Richardson, Yared Yearby and Wallace Richards joining our program, I probably wouldn't have gotten this great opportunity. Saying goodbye was tough but I was ready for the next step in my career!

During my first day on campus at Kent State, Antonio pulled up in his burgundy Rivera with a huge smile. I'll admit that having Antonio on the team made me feel more comfortable as I began my transition to college coaching. I knew I had my work cut out to make him better and more focused, but because of our prior relationship, I felt it would be simple. My goal was to make sure Jim started his head coaching career off with great success. Antonio and Anthony Wilkins were senior captains during my first season, both were helpful and remained coachable although I was new to the program. Anthony became my little brother and as we became closer it seemed we had some form of mental telepathy. Being able to relate to all of the players as I did at the high school level helped make the transition a bit smoother, but it was not without challenges.

Being at Kent State was a complete culture shock to me. Having been born and raised in a predominantly African-American city, I was not used to being a minority. Growing up, 95% of my teammates, classmates, teachers, administrators, and neighbors were black. I had attended a historically black college, and then moved back home to Detroit to teach and coach in an all-black environment. So, for the first twenty-seven years of my life, I was ONLY around black people, and had never experienced any racism in my life. And now, here I was living and working in Kent, Ohio where the population was predominately white. I went from being around all black people all the time to being the ONLY black person in the building.

"Man, I don't know if I can do this. I'm the only black person on staff in the program, and it seems like I'm the only black in the whole athletic department. I feel weird man, it's just different, I can't explain the feeling," I told Murray over the phone.

"Come on, Murph, you gotta hang in there, it can't be that bad. You will be ok" Murray replied.

Murray continued to encourage me and keep me focused on the future. As the season approached, scouting assignments were given to every staff member except for me. When this happened, I couldn't believe they wouldn't at least allow me to scout the exhibition games. Jim told me to team up with assistant coach, Rob Senderoff, to learn more about how to prepare a scouting report, our style of play and the system we were implementing into the program. After eight weeks of individual skill instruction and practice I felt I knew as much about our system as anyone. I could not help but to think this was happening because I was black. We had a great staff, all of which would eventually become Division I head coaches in their careers. Although I didn't draw any scouting assignments, I learned a ton by listening and taking notes. But all I could think of were the stories that everyone told me about why black people were hired in coaching positions at the college level. Black coaches are known to be good recruiters, and to have better relationships with the players when they arrived on campus. The incorrect and ignorant theory was that black coaches were only good for recruiting and not much else. I was experiencing the racist stigma of being "just a recruiter" and not a coach.

Recruiting, recruiting, and more recruiting was the only task that I received. Never mind the fact that I was a college graduate with six years of teaching experience. Forget the fact that I had coached teams to the state championships, and had multiple winning seasons. I was not considered capable enough to put together a scouting report for a Division I opponent. What I felt was unfair treatment made me even more eager to defy the label of being "just a recruiter." For hours at a time, I would watch film of our opponents and then study the scouting reports, regardless of the fact that it was not my job to do so. After gathering all of the information about our opponents, I'd bring several players to my office or stop by their hotel rooms on the road, to discuss, in detail, what I felt needed to be echoed for us to be successful.

I wasn't allowed to talk in official team film sessions, so this would be the only way my voice would be heard from a coaching perspective. It was also a way to gain more respect from the players as a coach, and not just as the "cool black guy" on the staff. I designed these meetings so that the players thought I was sent by Coach Christian to do them. I made sure to always reemphasize his message within mine because I wanted to add support, and not diminish the voice of the head coach. Taking this approach helped me create my own little niche with the players. This in turn kept my coaching skills sharp, and also furthered our position to win.

By now, recruiting was second nature to me; I could do it in my sleep. I showed my value to the program right away by keeping our current recruits intact, DeAndre Haynes and Cliff Brown while inviting a host of top players from the state of Michigan to visit the Kent State campus. Those statewide relationships in Michigan, along with the national relationships I built, were a tremendous additive to my performance at Kent State.

After getting over the initial culture shock, my first season at Kent State was such a fun ride. We won the MAC East regular season championship, and made it to the championship game of the MAC tournament in Cleveland, Ohio. I believe the only thing that stood in the way of us winning that championship was a knee injury that hindered Antonio's performance. Even though we lost in the championship game to Central Michigan, who had MAC player of the year Chris Kaman, we received a postseason bid to play in the National Invitation Tournament (NIT). We lost in the first round of the NIT but we had a great season. Jim was determined to keep the winning tradition going that was established by Gary Water and Stan Heath.

Shortly after the season, Antonio was in decision-making mode, and was sold on trying to play basketball at the NBA level or somewhere in Europe. I knew neither would be an option for him. It would be very tough for Antonio to get a legit opportunity to play in the NBA, so I tried to turn his focus toward football. He didn't realize it, but I had been working to get him in a position to play professional football for several months. In fact, the summer before his last basketball season, Antonio was asked to play football for Kent, but Jim and I talked him out of it. Agents warned Antonio that if he didn't play football at Kent while he was eligible, he wouldn't have the necessary footage for scouts to evaluate him to be considered an NFL prospect. Once he decided NOT to play football at Kent because of Jim's and my advice, I knew we HAD to do something to put him in position to at least have a chance to play football.

Coach Senderoff and I came up with a brilliant idea. We put together a letter on Antonio's behalf and sent it to all thirty-two NFL teams, introducing him and his interest in trying out after his senior season of basketball at Kent. We never told Antonio about this letter because we wanted him to concentrate strictly on basketball until the season wrapped up.

After the season came to an end, Antonio had very high hopes of playing in the NBA. Because he was invited to the Portsmouth Invitational pre-draft camp, Antonio believed he had a great chance to play in the NBA. I knew he had no chance, but I did not want to discourage his hopes right away. I advised Antonio to give Portsmouth a legit chance, but we agreed that if he did not leave there as one of the top three players, he should turn his attention to football. I explained to Antonio that six NFL teams had called me because of the letter we sent out. The teams had interest in visiting our campus to watch him run routes and catch the football. We both agreed that if Portsmouth did not go good, he would shift his focus.

He returned the following week, and as I predicted, he was not one of the top three players there, so we began setting up his NFL workouts from the Kent State basketball office. I was literally playing agent/Coach Murphy for about six months. I set up every workout and talked with every team interested throughout the draft and free agent process. Eventually, we decided Antonio would sign with the San Diego Chargers because of the tight end coach, Tim Brewster. Coach Brewster's attention to detail, his visits to campus, and his undying belief in Antonio's ability to play at the NFL level surpassed every other team. Antonio was soon on the fast track to stardom, and has never looked back.

Before I arrived at Kent State, I was single. My relationship with Shun took a great deal of energy from me both physically and emotionally, so I knew I needed to avoid the same mistake. I vowed that the next woman I became serious with had to have a clear understanding of how my career would affect certain aspects of our relationship. If she didn't, it would be a no go for me. Meeting a person who you're compatible with is already a challenge in itself. For me, finding that and a person who would be willing to take a backseat to my career at times, felt close to impossible!

Earlier in the season, Shun contacted me to see if we could give our relationship one last shot. After spending time talking to her on the phone, we agreed for her to come visit me in an attempt to spark an old flame. I was still single and thought now might be a better time in both of our lives, so I said, "why not?" The one thing that I always felt I wouldn't be able to deal with was the fact that Shun did not care for sports at all but I tried to have an open mind. So, the following week Shun drove to Stow, Ohio with her friend Connie to spend a couple of days with me. I didn't agree with her bringing Connie, but she insisted because she didn't feel comfortable driving up alone. After they arrived, we went to dinner, caught up, laughed, and had a good time. The following morning, I left for the office with positive thoughts and feelings. I worked for half of the day and returned back home around 1p.m., knowing they would only be there for one more night.

When I walked into my place, Connie was very upbeat with her usual smile, but I sensed an attitude from Shun. I couldn't figure out if something was actually wrong, or whether Shun was just being bratty about me having to go into the office earlier. I tried to lighten the mood in a few different ways, but nothing was working. After sitting in the living room talking with both of them, Shun asked if she could she speak with me in private. When we got to my bedroom, I tried to hug her.

"Get your hands off me!" she exclaimed.

I was stunned. "What's going on Shun? What did I do?"

I went into this long explanation about why I had to go into the office because I thought that was her problem.

"Who is Lisa?" she demanded.

"Lisa? Lisa, ummmmm, why are you asking me that?"

"I went through your drawers and saw a letter and picture she mailed to you," Shun said angrily.

I explained that Lisa was a friend I'd never met in person, who lived in Denver; I met her through my kinsman Lance.

"You're lying. Why would she say how much see loves you and can't wait to see you then, if y'all never seen each other?" she pressed.

"Shun, that's what my conversation does to women, but I promise I have yet to see Lisa in person," I said.

"It's cool, I'm sorry I came here. Connie, let's go! I can't do this!"

I tried to talk Shun out of it, but then it dawned on me. This was not meant to happen. Shun and I stayed in contact a while after that, but we never got back to the point of visiting each other. A few months later, she called me out of the blue one morning and asked if I had time to talk. I was driving from Kent State to Dayton for the Flyin' to the Hoop basketball tournament at the time. After the brief hello and small talk, Shun finally got to the point.

"Hey, I have something to tell you," she said.

My heart sank.

She paused, hesitated, then slowly uttered, "I don't know how to say this...," before starting to cry. "Maybe I'll call you later."

"NO, I'm driving, this is the perfect time to talk. What's going on? Are you okay?"

"Yes," she said.

"Well, then what, Shun? Spit it out! Do you have a boyfriend or something? It's okay," I said.

After a long pause she finally spit it out. "I'm pregnant."

"Oh, wow... wow. Are you going to keep it?" I asked.

"I'm getting married to the father, and yeah, we're gonna keep the baby," she said.

"Well, congratulations, I'm happy for you Shun."

I ended the conversation as positively as I could, and genuinely wished the best for her. But when I hung up, reality set in, and it hurt. Even though I knew deep down we weren't right for each other, it still didn't completely sit well with me that she was really moving on, leaving no possibility for us in the future.

I called Shun to check on her a month later, and asked if I was invited to the wedding; of course, I was not. On April 26, 2003, I drove to Detroit to recruit, with plans of being a wedding crasher. I found out the date, time, and location of Shun's wedding, and then asked Murray to come with me. I needed to get the full visual of this, so I could completely move on. I walked into the church, and everyone I knew was shocked to see me, but I came in with the most positive and supportive energy. As Shun walked down the aisle, I could tell when she saw me, she got nervous. During her vows she seemed uncertain, but happy. I walked through the receiving line, gave Shun a hug, and shook her husband's hand like a champ.

Even though I was truly happy for her, a pain still crept in my heart when I left the church that day. Murray insisted that we go out that evening just to get my mind off things, and I agreed. As we were walking into a private party at a lounge called Half Past Three, two women were entering the door at the same time as us. Murray jokingly said to one of the women, "Why are you staring at my boy? You like what you see? Ask him for his number, it's all good." Leave it to Murray to put a smile on everyone's face. We all shared a laugh before I got acquainted with the beautiful stranger.

The woman Murray was talking to was named TeNesha Handley. She was petite with gorgeous brown skin and a smile that lit up the room, just like my mother's. After Murray's embarrassing introduction, we started talking. She was really standoffish in the beginning, assuming I was like the typical Detroit guy she had probably met a million times before. About five minutes into the conversation, I could tell she was interested. I jokingly told her that night that she'd probably be my wife one day. Since she wouldn't give me her number, I gave her my business card. The next day, around 11:30 a.m. when I was driving back to Kent State, my phone rang and it was TeNesha. We ended up talking for about forty minutes, and my intuition told me that this would turn into a thrilling romance. After we hung up the phone, I arrived back on campus with a smile on my face, ready to prepare for summer recruiting.

It was time for a break now that the season was complete, spring recruiting was over and our seniors were set with the next steps of their careers. I enjoyed coaching on the college level but it came with a world of stress. I needed to let loose! For years, I was told Miami, Florida was a perfect spot for a fun getaway. So, I arranged a guys' trip with Murray, and another friend of ours, Kareem Hailey. The tickets were booked and our first annual Miami trip began.

"Party in the city where the heat is on. All night, on the beach till the break of dawn. Welcome to Miami, bienvenidos a Miami," Will Smith's song was the only one in my head. As soon as I saw the beautiful white sand beaches from the plane window, I knew this trip would be exactly what I needed. On the way to the hotel, we rode down Ocean Drive. There were luxury cars in the brightest colors, and too many gorgeous women to count. We walked into our one-bedroom suite in the Courtyard Marriott like we were doing it big. We threw down our bags, went straight to the infamous Wet Willie's, and then discovered the trendy Clevelander hotel, pool and patio.

The sun was setting, and it was time to hit the scene. Opium was the hottest club in Miami, so we HAD to be there. While in line, we found out there was a guest list. Hoping for the best, we thought we'd get lucky and get in with no issue. When we got to the front, they tried to turn us away because they didn't see our names. Things weren't looking good until Murray pushed us aside and pretended to be football player Antwan Smith, a running back for the New England Patriots. Just like that, we got in the club, landed in the VIP section, and continued the theme for the night. Murray, posing as Antwan, attracted the most beautiful women in the place.

At our table, the bottle girls insisted we take shots, and when I refused to have one, they wouldn't let up. This brought attention to the fact that I didn't drink. Growing up in an environment where there was excessive drug and alcohol abuse turned me off from ever wanting to drink or smoke. It was just not for me. Later the night when everyone was tipsy, I was ready to leave but no one wanted to stop partying. While I was waiting around, I struck up a conversation with the DJ.

"Not feelin' it tonight, huh?" the DJ asked.

"Oh, no, no... I'm just tired. Ready to get out of here. We been here all night, but the music is great, you're doing your thang, brotha," I said.

"Thanks, man. Here, take a copy of my mix tape," he offered.

"Oh, you're a rapper?"

"Nah, man. I'm not a rapper. I'm a musician," he said.

That DJ was Kanye West, who went on to become iconic.

Because our first Miami experience was so epic, we continued to go back every year after, adding on new members. It became an addiction to us all, and each year came with an upgraded experience. From mopeds to yachts, the Clevelander to Mr. Chow, the Courtyard to the W, Miami never let us down.

In order to continue the level of winning that was started at Kent State years ago, our staff had to put all the right pieces in place. The challenge of this particular year was that we had to start from scratch, and when considering different recruits, we had to determine the impact each player could make for the long run of our program. Losing our seniors, Antonio and Anthony, was hard for everyone, but extremely tough for me because we became so close, had a great year and almost won the MAC championship. After a good summer of recruiting and fall workouts, we were ready. We scored big with a great recruiting class. The options for continued success couldn't have been better!

We added freshman, Scott Cutley, from Los Angeles, and sophomores, DeAndre Haynes and Cliff Brown. They were paired with leaders of the new senior class, Eric Haut, John Edwards, Brian Bedford, and Matt Jakeway. The opportunity couldn't be greater with this set of guys who each had something to prove.

I could tell that I was becoming a better coach throughout the season, because I knew exactly what Jim expected and wanted from our staff. I understood our offense and the spacing it took for us to execute each set, and I was knowledgeable about the different wrinkles in each action. All of the terminology and schemes were becoming second nature to me now that I fully understood how important the details were to having a successful program at the college level. It took an entire season for me to be able to identify the different nuances at this level but with determination and willingness to learn, eventually you'll master your craft.

In my second season at Kent State, our players led us back to the MAC championship game, but we fell short again. More importantly, we had continued the culture of excellence at Kent and were in position to compete for championships in the years to come. Regardless of the loss in the championship game, it was an exciting time for Kent State basketball. We ended up receiving a bid to the NIT again which was a great accomplishment for our staff and a fresh group of guys. For the following season, we signed a great group of incoming players which included junior college All-American Jay Youngblood, Issac Knight, and Marcus Crenshaw, who were all from Detroit, and Mike Scott, from Indianapolis. "Tradition Never Graduates" is the Kent State mantra and something we were in position to continue.

Along with the success on the court, my relationship with TeNesha continued to flourish that year. Although she lived in Rochester Hills, Michigan, and we saw each other every other weekend. Being with her was unlike any other situation I had ever experienced. Our relationship just worked. We had differences, of course, but overall, being with TeNesha just felt right. We were happy, and she seemed to understand how important my career was to me. After meeting her parents and family, my feelings for her intensified even more. "TeNesha is the one, I think I'm gonna marry her," I would tell my inner circle, and it seemed that everyone in my life agreed that TeNesha was THE one for me. Our staff at the time seemed to think we were the perfect couple. Rob Senderoff told me TeNesha was a no brainer and so did the other staff members. TeNesha spent lots of time with wives during her visits to Kent. As they all became closer friends the pressure was on!

"It's time to grow up, Murph. Don't miss out on something great messing around," Rob Senderoff would say.

With my career on the rise, I believed that settling down was the right thing to do. Plus, I wanted this for myself. I always wanted to have a family and be there for my children one day. At the end of the day, I was the best version of myself with TeNesha by my side. TeNesha had grown up in a military household, which was quite the opposite of mine. Because of this, I knew I needed to properly ask her father, Woodie Handley, for his permission to have her hand in marriage. The ride up to their house in Rochester Hills was nerve wracking. I mean, what if he said no? I didn't actually think he would, but man, was I nervous. I kept it very clean and simple when I walked in with the message that day, and it went very well. Without a doubt in their hearts, our union would be one they would stand by. I had her parents' blessing. And a week later, I was designing the perfect engagement ring.

I decided the perfect day to propose on Valentine's Day. It was February 14th, 2004 at a restaurant called Pier W in downtown Cleveland, Ohio. I was anxious at the dinner table as I mentally prepared to ask TeNesha to marry me. Toward the end of the dinner, I had the waiter bring out the ring as if it was dessert. TeNesha was shocked when I proposed to her that night. She cried and said yes without hesitation. I was officially engaged. We debated about a wedding date before deciding to get married in May of 2005. She was happy about where we were headed, and so was I. Neither of us could have predicted that our lives were about to drastically change.

One calm summer day as I was sitting in my office organizing recruitment lists, my cell phone rang. When I looked to see who it was, the caller ID read private. Generally, I didn't pick up blocked or private calls, but something in me was curious this time.

"Hello," I said with hesitation.

"Murph, what's up? Did I catch you at a bad time? This is Troy Weaver."

"Hey! No, no the time is fine. Um, is this Weave from Syracuse?"

"Yes, can you talk?"

"Sure! What's up Weave?"

"Gotta question for you. Are you interested in coming to Syracuse?" he asked.

"Uhhhhh, like what do you mean, like to work camp?" I replied.

"Look, I'm taking an NBA job in a few weeks with the Jazz, and I thought about you replacing me here at Syracuse," Troy said.

"Wait, what? Replace you at Syracuse University, like me work there?" I was genuinely astonished.

"Yeah, man!" Troy chuckles.

"What! I LOVE Syracuse!" I said emphatically.

"I'm in the decision-making process right now, so you gotta be ready to roll. Keep this to yourself because I haven't shared this with anyone, but I believe I can get you in here," he said.

"I would love to come to Syracuse, man! That would be unbelievable!" I exclaimed.

"Ok... I've been recruiting Eric Devendorf hard, Coach loves him, so I wanna make sure that still happens if you get the job," Troy noted.

"Devendorf is a layup, I can guarantee that will happen" I replied.

"Ok, cool Murph. We'll talk again soon. Be ready" Troy said

"Wow, man, thank you. Thanks for thinking of me. This is…it's unbelievable. Thank you!"

"Ok, sounds good," he said before hanging up.

No way! No fucking way! I was so glad I accepted that private call.

Chapter Eight

GO ORANGE
OR GO HOME

Weave and I met during the recruitment of Mo Ager when Syracuse had interest in him a couple years prior to this phone call. We also spoke a few times about whether or not Syracuse would have a shot landing a few players from Michigan, Eric Devendorf and talented swingman, Chris Douglas-Roberts a few months earlier. I knew both players from my time as a high school coach, and co-founder of the Michigan Hurricanes AAU program. Our paths crossed again a few times at the Final Four, where most of the college coaches in the country have meetings each year and gather to have a good time. Weave and I developed a solid rapport over a few years, but we weren't super tight, so when he called me about replacing him at Syracuse, I was shocked.

I sat in my office after hanging up the phone with Weave in complete disbelief. I thought to myself, "How could this be happening? When did I manifest this?" It was only a few years ago that I was coaching high school basketball and teaching at an elementary school. A year before that, I was the first person in my family to graduate college, and four years before that, I barely made it out of high school. I was almost killed trying to sell drugs, and my mother was murdered when I was thirteen. I had no solid upbringing, and had never even had a single conversation with my father.

So, how in the hell was this happening to me? When did I become so deserving of all of this? The moment smacked me in the face like a car airbag during a bad accident. Suddenly, I was trying to evaluate the steps that brought me to this point. Since I graduated from college, I was just along for the ride, with everything happening so fast. I had no time to marvel at how extraordinary my life was becoming. Yes, I was working hard. But my passion for basketball never made it feel like actual work. Yes, I believed in myself, but I never saw this coming. I never imagined any of this for myself! Getting to Kent State was a dream, and I worked to my fullest potential every day. I attempted to work harder than anyone else. But I had no idea that things could get even better.

Now and then, we all hear the saying that "everything happens for a reason." That there is such a thing as fate. We each spend our lifetime trying to create and navigate the life path we want, with the awareness that some higher power has already mapped out the plan, regardless of our own ideas. The events in my life were leading me somewhere to do something big, but I wasn't exactly sure what that was just yet.

When Weave called me with the news that he wanted me to replace him at Syracuse, I was stunned. Not only was it completely unexpected, but because Syracuse University was my all-time favorite college basketball team and had been for quite some time. It was my dream school. For years, I watched them play and imagined what it would be like to be part of such a renowned program. And now, I was on the doorstep, waiting to be let in.

I could not sleep at all that night. Hall of Fame Coach, Jim Boeheim, would be calling my boss, Coach Jim Christian, the next day to let him know he was interested in me for a coaching position at Syracuse. Similar to a child on Christmas Eve, I tossed and turned all night, eager for the morning to come. A tremendous opportunity was on the brink of happening! The next day I arrived at the office earlier than I ever had. I attempted to go over my recruiting list, but was too anxious for Jim to get the call. Finally, Coach Christian knocked on my office door. My heart sped up as he popped in with the biggest grin on his face.

"So, you wanna leave us for the Cuse, Murph? Coach Boeheim just called me about you. Sounds like you're gonna interview at Syracuse this week. I spoke with Troy as well; he's highly recommending you as his replacement."

Wow! It was actually happening. This was really real. I was actually going to be considered for an assistant coaching position at Syracuse University!

"Syracuse is your favorite team; your dream school," Coach Christian said.

"I know. I cannot believe it. I'm praying this happens, Coach," I said.

"I'm really happy for you, and hope it does, too," he said sincerely.

About thirty minutes later, my phone rang displaying a 315-area code. It was THE Coach Jim Boeheim.

"Rob, Coach Boeheim, how are you?"

"I'm pretty good, Coach, especially now that I'm hearing from you. Did you get the note I sent you about my Lakers beating the Spurs in the playoffs?"

"Yes, I did, the Lakers were lucky," he said before we both laughed. "Hey, we wanna bring you in this Thursday to talk about you joining us in Syracuse. Does the date work for you?"

I tried to sound cool but eager at the same time when I replied, "Yes, that day works perfect!"

"Good, Troy will call you to work out travel, and we'll see you soon," Coach Boeheim said.

"Sounds good, Coach, thanks for the call and I'll see you soon."

I had just spoken to the legendary Coach Jim Boeheim! I could not believe it!

Within an hour of the call, Troy was arranging my travel to Syracuse University.

"As long as you don't blow the interview, the job is yours. You don't have to wear a suit, come relaxed. Boeheim doesn't get caught up in presentation. He knows what he wants, so you'll be good. He's also excited about Devendorf and getting back into the Detroit area to recruit, so that helps as well."

I could barely sleep in the days leading up to the interview. That Wednesday, I drove to Detroit to share the exciting news with my family and TeNesha. They were all thrilled at the opportunity, and knew how huge this would be for my career. The following morning, I was up bright and early, dressed in a suit with an orange and blue tie, headed to the Detroit airport. I spent the entire flight reviewing talking points in my head, making sure I didn't leave out any notable things that would make me the best man for the job. Upon exiting the Syracuse airport, Troy was parked right outside waiting to pick me up. We headed straight to the office at the Manley Fieldhouse.

"Troy, is there anything else you think I may need to say to Coach?" I asked.

"Murph, just be yourself, the job is yours. Just be cool," replied Troy.

Fifteen minutes later, we pulled up to an oddly shaped building. As I walked in, I couldn't help but notice it was fully encompassed in orange and blue. You could feel the pride of the school immediately. There were plaques and trophies and honors all on display as we walked through the lobby. I sat and took in the moment as I waited for Boeheim's assistant to call me in. Five minutes later, it was time.

"Rob, how are you?" Coach Boeheim said.

I was still in awe. There I was, face-to-face, with one of my coaching idols, a true legend of college athletics, James Arthur Boeheim. The pictures, trophies, plaques, signature balls, and memorabilia throughout his office blew me away. Coach Boeheim discussed the job duties and recruitment expectations for the position. He then briefly went over the salary, and shortly after he said, "Welcome to Syracuse."

I could not BELIEVE IT! I had just landed an hour ago, and was already hired… at least I thought so.

"Thanks, Coach. I'm happy to be here!" I said.

After I shook his hand, I got up to leave his office and was slightly confused. Wait, was he saying I was hired? Or just welcoming me to the town? His assistant then walked me back to Troy's office, and asked him to take me down to meet Jake Crouthamel, who was then the Athletic Director (AD).

"Congrats, man! You can relax now!" laughed Troy.

I couldn't believe it! It was actually happening. I met with the AD, Coach Bernie Fine, and Coach Mike Hopkins before checking into the Sheraton Hotel on campus. After accepting the position, I had a media interview with Kim Baxter of the Syracuse Post Standard newspaper. Kim along with her colleague, Mike Waters, did a great job of welcoming and introducing me to the Syracuse community.

Later that evening, I had dinner with the staff at Scotch and Sirloin. Coach's wife, Juli Boeheim, stopped by the dinner and seemed to give her approval of me right away. When she found out that TeNesha was from her home state of Kentucky, that brought a smile to Juli's face. The dinner was perfect. Everyone welcomed me with open arms, and was excited for the talent and relationships I would add to our team and staff. At the conclusion of the dinner, I was formally inducted into the Orange family.

When I returned to my hotel room that night, I called everyone I knew to let them know the news. I was officially an assistant coach for the Syracuse University basketball program, working under the great Jim Boeheim! The following day, I signed all of the necessary paperwork with HR, and visited with Dan Shworles, the Syracuse basketball equipment manager, to get some recruiting gear for the road. Before I headed back to the airport, Troy decided to take me around Syracuse and introduce me to a few people I should know. The first person he called was Dennis Duval, the chief of police in Syracuse who was about to retire. If anything ever went down in the Cuse and you needed to get to law enforcement, he would be the one to call. The second stop was in the hood, to visit his barbershop. I knew I would never need a haircut because I'd been rockin' the bald lifestyle since the ninth grade when I had a mishap with the guard on my clippers, but I needed to know the frontrunners in the hood. Carl Newton was the neighborhood enforcer and go-to guy for all things happening in this part of town. Our final stop, which looking back was the most important stop, was to meet Giovanna McCarthy, the owner of Paparazzi Day Spa. Paparazzi is the best salon in the Syracuse area and were I visited for facials, manicures, pedicures and good massages. Giovanna and I built a great relationship that has lasted since the day we met 15 years ago. She's one of the most loyal and supportive people I've ever met!

After our visit with Giovanna, I headed back to the airport to close out my tenure at Kent State. Coach Christian called a meeting in his office with the entire team when I returned to announce and celebrate my departure. And before I could get out a single word, tears came rolling down my face (yes, I am a crier, as you should be able to tell by now). I had so many mixed emotions when surrounded by the staff and players. I was extremely happy for where I was going, but equally sad about leaving the place where I started my college coaching career.

We had just recruited three players from Detroit, which I played a major role in landing, and they had just moved in on campus a week prior. I could see the disappointment in the eyes of the team when they heard the news. But joy for what my future held, made them happy for me. One of the players noted it was the most inspiring moment he had been a part of in a while. There aren't many African-American men that get to this level in basketball, so he was right. Without much notice, I was inspiring the other young black men who stood before me. All I was concerned with at that moment was feeling like I let down the incoming class, which I heavily helped recruit. But even harder was letting down the parents of the guys I recruited, who were even more disappointed than their sons were. All in all, I received nothing but good wishes from everyone around me. It wasn't until I said goodbye to Kent State that I realized the magnitude of my impact. I had no idea I had touched so many people's lives in such a short span.

After I left Kent State, it was time to get back to business. While I was in Detroit, I went to see Will Smith, a childhood friend who was a coach and now a vice president of the Michigan Hurricanes AAU team. I hoped to put a plan in place for Devendorf to commit to Syracuse at the ABCD camp the following week. I knew if I could walk into Syracuse with a McDonald's All-American as my first recruit, I would be off to a phenomenal start. Needless to say, Eric was sold on Syracuse, and so was his family and Will Smith. The word in Detroit and around the country spread very quickly. "Murph is the new assistant coach at Syracuse!" I pinched myself everyday hoping this wasn't just a dream.

After the July Fourth holiday, I met up with the Syracuse staff on the road to start recruiting. My first stop on the trail was with Coach Boeheim in Indianapolis, IN for the Nike All-American Camp. The first player I took Coach Boeheim to evaluate was Chris Douglas-Roberts (CDR). He had great length, versatility and athletic ability. My instincts told me CDR could be a perfect addition to the program. CDR was a long point guard who stood 6'7", and I believed if paired him with Devendorf, they could become a very electric backcourt for the future of Syracuse basketball. CDR could also play the top and back of the 2-3 zone very effectively.

"He can't shoot. You need to be a good shooter to be an effective playing guard," said Coach Boeheim.

"Coach, but he can do everything else pretty well, and he's also tough," I said. "We can improve his shooting, and he can play the front and back of the zone," I added.

Although this was the first player we were evaluating together, I felt the need to let Coach Boeheim know how much I believed CDR could help us. Because I had such a strong belief, Coach Boeheim agreed to reevaluate him. We went back that evening to watch CDR again, and he didn't play well. Much to Coach Boeheim's point, he shot the ball from the outside poorly. After watching CDR that night, I knew I had no chance convincing Boeheim of his skill. Deep down, I knew in my heart CDR was very good, but I was the new kid on the block and had to prove myself to gain Coach's trust. CDR would have committed to Syracuse right away had we pulled the trigger. With the current roster and solid commits in place we felt we should go in another direction. If I could go back in time, I would have pushed extremely hard for Coach Boeheim to offer CDR a scholarship because I felt he was the perfect fit and he was from my hometown of Detroit.

As it turned out, CDR ended up playing at Memphis, and went on to become a First Team All-American, named First Team Conference USA, selected to the All-Freshman Team, and played for a national championship. Even though I was right, I knew I had to be patient in my new role. As I mentioned, in time Boeheim's trust in me would change, but let's not skip too far ahead.

I shifted my focus to the younger guys at the Nike camp that year. Those guys included Kevin Durant, DeShawn Sims, Donte Greene, Raymar Morgan, Chris Knight, Durrell Summers and Herb Pope. After evaluating numerous players again, the following morning, we departed the Nike camp to fly to Teaneck, New Jersey for the ABCD Camp. Eric Devendorf, Will Smith, and Chris Grier-Luchy all awaited our arrival. Shortly after

THE LIFE OF ROB MURPHY

navigating through the opening day at ABCD camp, Devendorf announced his commitment to Syracuse. I was on the job five days, and we received a commitment from a Top 20 player in the nation, who would be a McDonald's All-American. Congrats from my fellow staff poured in for landing such a huge accomplishment so quickly.

The talent at ABCD camp was off the charts, as usual! I was able to get a detailed evaluation of the players, but the talent from court-to-court was completely overwhelming. Greg Oden, OJ Mayo, Bill Walker, Monta Ellis, Daequan Cook, Derrick Caracter, Gerald Green, Amir Johnson, Andre Blatche, Curtis Kelly, Lance Thomas, Dallas Laurderdale, and Marcus Johnson were just some of the phenomenal players that I evaluated at ABCD camp that year.

There was so much talent in the room that I misevaluated one of our own Hurricane players, Wilson Chandler. Will Smith begged me to bring him to Syracuse with Eric. Coach Boeheim and Coach Hopkins liked Wilson as well, but I felt we could get a more promising player at the time. Wilson was a quiet guy, unassuming, and not very aggressive. Yes, he did have the size and ability, but I was caught up in getting the best of the best at the time. I wanted to bring in the McDonald All-Americans who would become pros in one to two years, which was the incorrect approach when sustaining a program in the long run.

Troy Weaver established his legacy by recruiting Carmelo Anthony to Syracuse, and that was the only caliber of player I was after at this moment. In addition, Wilson wasn't scoring much at the camp, and his stock plummeted. I learned a huge lesson from this mistake. I truly misevaluated Wilson. What made all of this worse is Wilson would have definitely committed to Syracuse. There would not have been much of a recruiting process because of the connection and our history together. Wilson Chandler will always be the player I regret letting slip away. Chills race up my spine just imagining if Wilson joined us with all of the talent we already had in place at the time.

Wilson went on to become a First Round draft pick in the NBA, and is having a great career as a professional player to this day.

> It's always a good practice to acknowledge when you are wrong. It allows you to be open to learning another point of view, which widens your own perspective. The phrase, "I apologize, I was wrong," or "I may be wrong," has diverted many conversations throughout my life and career for the better. An honest self-evaluation is pivotal for growth.

We completed the 2005 recruiting class by landing an unknown player, Arinze Onuaku (AO). AO was rated the 223rd player in the country, but I knew he would make a huge impact at Syracuse. Big, strong, athletic, and tough with a half hook, he was all we needed to anchor our zone into the future.

AO's recruitment came down to Syracuse and the University of Georgia. After a great visit with us AO decided to visit Georgia the following weekend. AO called us from the airport on Sunday after his visit and told us he was committing to Syracuse. I was excited because I knew the potential in AO. Eric and AO became key contributors to the Orange program for the following five years. And for me, this will always be my favorite recruiting class during my time at the Cuse. AO and Eric were two totally different players, who played different positions, were different races, grew up in different environments, and had different expectations. Coaching both of them helped prepare me for any situation I would ever experience in recruiting for the remainder of my career. They both gave me a chance to prove myself as a recruiter by making an immediate impact at the highest level of college basketball.

When the July recruiting period came to a close, it was officially time for me to move to Syracuse. And before I knew it, September rolled around again. I was eager to meet our current team, and ready to compete for a national championship. We started the season ranked #5 in the country and was led by All-American forward, Hakim Warrick, and sharp-shooting guard, Gerry McNamara. These guys had already won a national title, so I knew we had a great chance to win.

During our first staff meeting, Coach Boeheim made it clear that it was my job to get the forwards ready through individual workouts in the pre-season. Coach Christian had coached every workout and practice at Kent State, so this was new for me. I finally had my chance to work directly with the players without the control of the head coach dictating my every step. Wow! LET'S GO! I was refreshed and fired up by the news that I would get to work with the forwards. I immediately put a plan in place and got down to business.

Chapter Nine

A DREAM

"Good morning, Syracuse! We are gearing up for pre-season in college sports, and today we have the newest assistant coach of the Orange basketball team, Rob Murphy, here in the studio for the very first time. What's happening Rob? Welcome to the Cuse," announced Dr. Rick Wright.

"Thanks, Dr. Wright, I'm happy to be here," I said into the mic.

"For all you listeners out there who don't know, Coach Murphy joins the Orange alongside a very impressive recruiting class, which he himself has brought on with All-American Eric Devendorf, who will probably be in our starting lineup this season. Rob, tell us how you managed to land a McDonald's All-American in your first forty-eight hours as a new assistant coach with the Orangemen?"

"Well, Eric and I are both natives of Michigan. Eric also played for the Michigan Hurricanes AAU program that I helped create years ago with longtime friends, Chris Grier-Luchey and Ra Murray. I wanted to land a great player from my home state, and felt Eric would be a great match for Coach

114

Boeheim and Syracuse basketball. Gerry McNamara's success also helped Devendorf visualize the type of college career he could have. If he follows in his foot-steps he can potentially become the next great guard to play for the Orange," I explained.

"Wow, amazing... well, I think I speak for the entire Orange Nation when I say we are extremely excited for the upcoming season, and happy to have you on the team. We'll be right back with more from Coach Rob Murphy after this break," Dr. Wright said before going to commercial.

My plan was simple: become the top recruiter in the country. And to do that, I would need to utilize all the relationships I built to help us get in front of the best players in the nation.

There will always come a time in your life when you will without a doubt need the help of others to help push you ahead. I cannot reiterate enough how important other people have been to my own success. Understand early on that every relationship you foster along your journey has the potential to be imperative to your career. You never know who will have the ability to work a life-changing miracle in your favor. That's why you should always be kind, and do what you can for others, when you can. The truth is, you can't do it all by yourself. There are very few careers, if any, that revolve around a single person. The sooner you realize you don't know it all, that you don't have all the answers, and that YOU, YES, EVEN YOU, need help, the closer you will be to reaching the top. Before I even got to the Syracuse campus, I already accomplished a huge goal for the program, and this was all because of relationships. The strength of this one relationship helped me to get to a coaching position at my dream school.

The stage was set when I finally stepped foot in the Manley Fieldhouse gym for our first pre-season practice. I immediately meshed with the staff, who already had so much respect for what I brought to the table. Can you believe that every member on the Syracuse Basketball staff went to school at Syracuse, except me? When I realized this, I was floored. Over an eleven year span, Troy and I were the only non-Syracuse alum who worked for Coach Boeheim. How that happened, I have no idea!

Bernie Fine was in his twenty-ninth season with Coach Boeheim, and responsible for coaching the centers. He was very hands-on academically as well. Allen Griffin was the Director of Basketball Operations and a former Syracuse Player. Opposite of me was fifth year Assistant Coach, Mike Hopkins. Hop and I would be the two top lead assistants. Before the first practice, I deeply researched Coach Boeheim's style of coaching and history with players to see how my methods could compliment this.

Some of the best advice I was given and will give to all of you is, strive to be the most knowledgeable person in the room. Know everything about what you're doing and interested in, and know it front to back. I spent hours studying this program and all the roles and key players involved as much as I could before I actually started, and that put me ahead immediately. My first step in becoming a great recruiter was to know something about every player rated in the top 150 in the country. It's your job to become the information bank, know the answers before the questions are asked. Knowledge is Power!

All this knowledge led me to one question: "What do I bring to the table that no one else in the Syracuse basketball program does?" My research didn't end until I could find that answer. And eventually it came to me as I was observing on the first day. What I brought to the program that no one else did was ME! That's it! There was no one else in that gym who mirrored or even came close to my life experiences, and the only people in the entire gym who shared the same skin color as me were the majority of our players, and the director of basketball ops.

In fact, I had more in common with the players than the rest of the staff. And the funny thing about it was, no one knew. No one was aware of my background or what I had been through growing up in Detroit. And I felt it was in my best interest to keep it that way because I didn't want my past to be judged and adversely affect my future. By just using myself, I would automatically add to the dynamic of the team because I had something no one else could offer. I didn't realize it at the time, but this detail would help carry me throughout my entire career.

Understanding the various personalities that made up our team was very important when trying to maximize our talent and blend our players into a cohesive unit. Pre-season workouts started early at 6:00 a.m., and I had individual meetings with each player so I could begin to get to know everyone. Next, we had individual instruction lasting forty minutes per group. I was responsible for the most important position of the Orange program, the forwards. The forwards have always had a huge responsibility defensively. Over the past twenty-nine years, the forwards have led Syracuse in scoring and rebounding 90% of the time.

Hakim Warrick was the first forward I met with. Hakim was a senior captain who we had high expectations for the up-coming season. He had a great three years before my arrival, but we wanted his senior season to be extraordinary. We spoke at length about how I could help improve his game. His outside shot needed to become more consistent, and his mid-post attack needed to be more fluent. We worked daily on making those outside shots and attacking the rim using the dribble from the mid-post. There was potential for him to be Big East player of the year.

As workouts continued, I started to discover the commitment level of each player. Certain players had more mental discipline than others. This trait is imperative to know once the season kicked in, because mentality and approach is half the battle to winning and being consistently successful.

> Who you ultimately become in life is dictated by your mentality and mindset. The way you think affects the way you act. The way you act impacts what you do, the people you meet, who you build relationships with, and the opportunities that present themselves. The mind is more powerful than any of us truly understand.
>
> We all have different dreams, goals, and desires. But your mental make-up is what will separate you from others. The way you think will dictate everything happening around you, positive, negative and everything in between. How you overcome struggle will be dependent on your mentality. Your thoughts can hold you back if you aren't aware of them. Self-awareness is key. If you want something, you have to truly believe that you can attain it.
>
> Your energy and belief is very important. To create the energy and belief you will need to be successful, it will always start and end with your mindset. If you think positively and envision that you can attain your goal, then eventually that vision will take form. Change your mind, and you can change your entire life.

Hak, Terrance Roberts (TRob), and, Dayshawn Wright were the forwards that season, and each of them worked hard consistently, not just physically, but mentally. During my seven years with Syracuse basketball, six of those years, a forward would lead us in scoring and rebounding. Mindset proved to be the key ingredient here.

Our first official practice marked the start of the college basketball season. The media swarmed the gym with an undercurrent of little murmurs as they keenly watched the new team warming up. Our top donors were observing as well. About ten minutes into pre-practice, the gym doors swung open, and in walked the legend himself, THE Head Coach of Syracuse University Men's Basketball, Jim Boeheim. Everything stopped in that single moment. The media conversations came to a hush, the warm ups took a pause, and everyone acknowledged Coach with a rush of applause.

I stood on the court watching my new boss command the attention of every single person in the gymnasium. I mean, the man had such regality about himself that even before he spoke, his energy alone demanded this acute attention. And that's when I thought to myself, "Wow, I am working with a sports legend." Like most super stars who have reached optimal freedom in their genius, Boeheim's aura exuded a grounded energy and confidence that could be felt by everyone in the room.

I would learn over the years that Coach had a very mysterious style and methodical way of approaching things. You could never really tell what he was actually thinking or how he felt, but somehow, he got his point across. I admired the fact that he was a man of very little words who said a lot. He was like the Wizard of Oz – glorified by the city of Syracuse and the basketball world. Boeheim implemented a defense that no one believed would work, and he's perfected it with success for over forty years. He reveled in proving the doubters wrong.

Coach Hop always brought a high level of energy that remained from the start to the end of practice. I've never seen anything like it. His energy was infectious, and it always got us all going. Bernie was the talker, always teaching, even though sometimes he spoke a bit too long as players wanted to get on the floor and compete. We stretched as a team, and then separated into twenty minutes of group work for every practice. After groups, we began going over our offensive sets and into 5-on-5 down and back action.

Hak and T Rob came out the gate strong as expected. They were prepared, ready to work hard, and competed every day. Dayshawn, on the other hand, struggled, as the majority of freshmen do. Everyone wants to make it to the NBA, so the pressure of being good right away sometimes causes friction. It took time for some freshmen to learn patience in their growth within the program. After seeing everyone go through the first two weeks of individual skill instruction, I understood why we had a chance to have such a special season. We had size and length at every position, and Gerry McNamara was undeniably one of the best guards in the country that year.

Practice was in full swing, the season was approaching, and from the outside, the Syracuse men's basketball family seemed cohesive from top to bottom. But as time passed, I started to encounter what happens on most coaching staffs; a power struggle among men with egos and hidden agendas.

As the new guy, I did my best to remain neutral and quietly observed all the action. With Troy leaving for the NBA, Hop quickly became the most important assistant coach, and was already the "Golden Child" of the program. Hop had earned the adulation of the city and fans, having played at Syracuse for Coach Boeheim, who treated him like a son. As the years went on, I learned how good and creative he was at manipulating things to get what he wanted. This served him and the program particularly well when it came to recruiting.

While I was getting familiar with the office politics, I became good friends with one of our assistant women's basketball coaches, Quintin Hillsman (Coach Q), who worked under Head Coach Keith Cieplicki. At the time, they had the worst team in the Big East conference. Coach Q, like myself, was a go-getter when it came to recruiting. I liked the fact that he was like a spark plug, and found a way to be positive in just about any situation. Being black assistant coaches, we faced some of the same challenges and were able to help each other out. A year later, Cieplicki stepped down and our athletic director, Daryl Gross eventually hired Q as the head coach. Not many believed he could change the landscape of the women's basketball program. But fourteen years later, he is working on a Hall of Fame head coaching career, and I believed in him the second he got the job.

The time had finally come for our first exhibition game of the season, and I still couldn't believe that I was an assistant coach at Syracuse University, alongside the famous Jim Boeheim. There were about 12,000 fans in the Carrier Dome, and there was an energy that I can hardly describe. Chills ran over my body as I walked out of the tunnel for tip off. "This isn't even a real crowd, Murph!" explained Griff, our Director of Basketball Operations. Wow, I knew I was in for a phenomenal experience.

After winning our first two home games I was able to make my first ever trip to NYC! We were playing in the Coaches vs Cancer tip-off classic held at Madison Square Garden, one of the greatest venues in all of basketball! "New York New York Big City of Dreams (Snoop Dogg voice)" I was excited to experience the lights of Time Square, play at MSG and taste the best pizza NYC had to offer. We knocked off Mississippi State in our first game then beat a talented Memphis team to bring home the early season champion-ship. We continued to roll as we started the season twenty and one! My first regular season ride was incredible! We won twenty-seven games, captured a Big East tournament championship, and our forward, Hakim Warrick, was named the MVP. Throughout the season, there were some ups and downs that contributed to our early exit out of the NCAA tournament that year. We had a few players that tested positive for marijuana use, which automat-ically eliminated them from playing, and our best guard was dealing with depression, which caused him to quit the team mid-year. Everyone critiqued our loss to Vermont, but on the inside, we knew exactly what contributed to this upset loss. In most cases it's bigger than forty minutes witnessed and remembered by media and fans.

When the season was over, I reflected on how far I'd come and the great experiences I had my first season in Orange. I learned so much working next to coach Boeheim. I came into the program totally believing that man-to-man defense was the best option, but by the end of the year, I understood the genius of Coach Boeheim and our zone defense. Coach Boeheim always has ultimate confidence in his players, especially on the offensive side of the ball. I learned that when dealing with players during the game, less is better. Boeheim taught me the importance of not over-coaching. Instead, it was imperative to put players in position to be successful while allowing them to play through mistakes. Because we were so experienced and had such talented players, it truly made my transition easy. My life and career had changed forever.

Going into the off- season, our focus shifted to recruiting. We were going to lose four senior leaders the following season, so we knew we had to start preparing to bring in a talented class with all the experience we would be losing. Hop and I met in June to figure out what our biggest needs would be, and the type of players we were looking for. The competition in the Big East conference was at an all-time high. We competed against the likes of UConn, Georgetown, Pittsburgh, and Villanova, which were all great programs with lots of talent. Not to mention Louisville and Marquette, both Final Four programs, who would join the Big East that same year. Hop and I felt we needed to be the best one-two punch in the recruiting game so we went to work.

Around this same time, TeNesha and I were also approaching our wedding date. Admittedly, I had been so consumed with making a good impression on Coach and trying to do everything I could to help us win, I wasn't giving a whole lot of attention to the wedding planning. A few trips back to Michigan was all that was needed, because TeNesha had everything handled with assistance from the wedding planner. The toughest time for TeNesha was when her mother bailed on her and decided not to help because TeNesha did not see things her way. Her mother did not believe in over spending on an elaborate wedding. TeNesha had a great vision, and I'm glad she stood her ground to make it a special day for everyone involved.

The night before the wedding, my groomsman and I went out in Detroit to a lounge, Half Past Three. When we got there, William Wesley, a.k.a. "World Wide Wes," also happened to be there, and was introduced to me. Wes is a power broker, and one of the most influential men in the business side of basketball. Wes is noted for his relationships with numerous high-profile NBA players, professional team owners and college basketball head and assistant coaches. It was not by mistake that I met Wes that night. He is known for his strength in connecting people to help them become successful while remaining successful himself. From that evening forward, we kept in touch and became friends.

Before I could catch my breath, it was finally time to marry the love of my life. On May 29, 2005, time slowed down when I watched her walk down that aisle. I could not believe what was happening for me. How in the world had I managed to be a coach at Syracuse University and have this radiant woman walking toward me in the most elegant white dress?! So many thoughts raced through my mind before she made it to the alter. I was excited and nervous all at the same time. If only my mother could be there with me at this moment; I know she was so happy for me.

As TeNesha continued walking toward me, my nerves slowly subsided. I knew in my heart that TeNesha was an incredible person who I loved. She was not only beautiful, she had a fantastic personality that exuded charisma and charm. We exchanged vows, and just like that, I was a married man! Our honeymoon destination was Aruba and needless to say, we had the time of our lives! You name it, we did it!

When I returned from my honeymoon, Hop and I came up with a plan to land our next two great recruiting classes, which needed to be stellar. We were close to landing top recruit, Paul (Dugga) Harris. We felt Paul would be as talented as any freshman in the country, but his recruitment was a chase that aged Hop 20 years! We knew that to continue the success of the program the 06' class needed to be good but the 07' classes needed to be great because of our graduating seniors. I remember July recruiting in Las Vegas, when Ra Murray decided to play one of the funniest pranks on Hop I ever witnessed. Ra felt he needed to lighten the mood as we (Hop, Ra and myself) were having lunch in between games. As we sat together eating at Fridays Ra called Hop's cell phone "The deal is off, Paul is going to Pitt, it's over" whispered Ra, "what, who is this, who is this, tell me who this is" frantically said Hop into his phone. Hop immediately jumped up from the table running toward the front door. I'm yelling "Hop Hop, come back, it's Ra, it's Ra" as Ra and I are laughing. Hop was so stressed over the recruiting process he didn't realize that Ra turned his body and called his cell as he was sitting right next to him! Once Hop calmed down and realized it was a prank call, Hop laughed "You Motherfuckers, damn Ra, you're fucking crazy man. You just gave me a heart attack, laughing". This was one of the funniest things I ever experienced! There were lots of twists and turns before Paul committed at the end of the summer, but we were pleased to have Paul and Mike Jones committed as our 06' recruiting class.

We decided to have an elite camp that would attract all the top high school players from the East Coast to come visit the Syracuse campus. And boy, did our plan work! That summer we had twins Markeiff and Marcus Morris, Antonio "Scoop" Jardine, Rick Jackson, and Dion Waiters, who were all from Philadelphia. Corey Fisher from New Jersey, Jonny Flynn, Tobias Harris, Mookie Jones, Kevin Jones, and Taylor Battle who were all from New York. Taylor King from California, Darquavous Tucker from Michigan, Rakim Sanders from Rhode Island, Tristen Thompson from Toronto, and Greg Echenique from New Jersey all attended the first ever Syracuse elite camp. The camp turned out to be extremely successful.

As we evaluated the talent, there were two players who stood out to me the entire forty-eight hours on campus. Jonny Flynn and Dion Waiters were those two players. They were very TOUGH and TALENTED. They each had the strength, quickness, and skill for the guard position. Listed at 6 feet tall, Jonny was a tad small for the Big East, but had all the other attributes to be successful. I immediately told Hop, "I know Paul is very good and he's the one we've been chasing, and I know Jonny is his younger teammate, but Jonny's the one! We need to extend an offer to him now, he's a must get!" Dion was a few years behind Flynn, but I gave Hop the exact same advice on Dion. Jonny was a coach's dream. He was talented, had great grades, and came from a solid upbringing. Dion on the other hand, would prove to be more of a challenge academically and socially. But I knew if he could overcome these obstacles, it would pay off greatly for Syracuse and Dion.

After camp, we hit the road to evaluate more players around the country. My first stop with Coach Boeheim was the Nike All-American camp in Indianapolis, IN. This is where we continued to evaluate Scoop Jardine, Manny Harris, and some of the other top guys throughout the country. This was also the first place I saw Donte Greene. Donte was under the radar and playing out of position (center), but after looking at his shooting ability and the way he moved, I believed he could be our next star forward. We had missed out on Kevin Durant the year before, so I was determined not to let another great forward from the DMV area (D.C., Maryland, Virginia) get away.

Donte, Michael Beasley, Nolan Smith, Austin Freeman, and Dar Tucker became my main targets, with Donte at the top of the list. I believed Donte would be the next KD or Rudy Gay. Although Mike Beasley was rated higher, there were academic concerns with him, so I shifted my focus to Donte. Donte had the skillset and ability, along with the charisma of a star athlete.

Coach Hop honed in on the guards, in pursuit of Jonny Flynn and Scoop Jardine. Although they were both point guards, we decided to recruit the two. Usually a program doesn't recruit two players in the same position in the same class. We only recruited both to make our chances greater of landing one of them. But Scoop, who was our second option, committed first, but we continued to recruit Jonny even after Scoops' commitment because he was just so talented. Hop was the man for the job. He is a hell of a salesman; he could convince a whale to buy water.

Things began to fall into place after Scoop broke the ice and announced his commitment. Rick Jackson would come next, then Greene to commit, Flynn commit, Sean Williams commit! The class was just about complete, and Cuse was in the House! We lost Mike Jones, who transferred back to South Carolina (one of my best recruiting jobs ever the prior year) after his first semester at Syracuse. Mike would have been in the NBA after his second year if he had a little patience. But he was home sick, and didn't deal well with the hype of Paul Harris and lack of playing time. Mike was just as talented, but he was the odd man out. With this loss, I was forced to turn to the junior college ranks to fill the last void. Coach Boeheim had no interest in junior college players, as he said these players usually came with more problems. "Murph, there's a reason they are in junior college," Boeheim said. But I wasn't listening.

I ended up hearing about a player named Kristof Ongenaet who was from Germany. He was playing at Cuesta junior college in California, and was under the radar. He only had one high-major offer, and a host of mid-major schools recruiting him. My decision to pursue Kristof turned out to be a perfect example of trusting your gut. In most cases, schools rely on seeing which other schools are recruiting a player to determine if he's worthy of playing in their program. While I am always aware of what the scouting report says and which other schools are offering scholarships, I focus more on my instincts when I'm evaluating a player.

So, what is instinct? The online Merriam-Webster dictionary defines it as the "tendency of an organism to make a complex and specific response to environmental stimuli without involving reason." The most important part of that definition is "not involving reason." Finding the value in these inner "knowings" before logic sets in and convinces us to follow reason and practicality is the challenge. But when you can listen to your instincts, you will benefit from their power. What makes me such a good recruiter is just that! I have a keen instinct for talent and what I feel the potential will be. If I don't get this feeling when I'm evaluating a player, I don't overthink it, I just move on. I have put my instincts into practice, and they have been verified over and over throughout my career.

After watching Kristof, I knew he would be the final player we needed. We had already put together an impeccable recruiting class, and I knew if I could sell Coach Boeheim on Kristof, he would be the icing on the cake. After sharing all of his background information and showing Coach Boeheim his highlight film, he gave me the go-ahead to bring Kristof on campus, and the rest is history. It's brings a smile to my face every time I think about Kristof's official visit to Syracuse. Mr. Ongenaet (Kristof's father) caught a taxi from NYC to Syracuse when he landed from Belgium. The family spoke little English so there was a breakdown in communication about travel and the connection flight to Syracuse. The Ongenaets' enjoyed their visit, and his son's overall experience with us at Syracuse went very well.

My second basketball season at Syracuse was a struggle throughout the regular season. We had plenty of talent, but very little experience and could not find any consistency. We couldn't pin down an effective point guard to play with Gerry in his role as our main scorer. It took us a long time to get into a steady flow. By season's end, we were playing awful basketball. I'll never forget the game when DePaul beat us by forty-plus points on national television. It was truly embarrassing and Coach Boeheim's worst loss of his career. The only great news that came during the season was when TeNesha and I found out we were expecting our first child.

So many different emotions surrounded the idea that I would soon be a father to this real-life little human. The fact that I had no relationship with my father made me very nervous about the whole idea. I wasn't sure what it actually took to be a dad because I had no prior experience to draw from. It scared me to know I really had no idea what I was supposed to do or how I was supposed to act. But even though I had no blueprint on how to be a father, I was most sure about one thing… I knew that no matter what obstacles I ran into, I would always be there. Period. Unlike my father, I would love, care for, and build a great relationship with my child. Having the chance to do that made me so happy. And I was even more overjoyed when I learned we were having a boy and he could possibility have the same birthday!

The Big East tournament arrived and Gerry gave us all new life! His game winning 3-point shot against Cincy kick-started the quest for our second straight Big East tournament title. It was one of the best performances in Big East tournament history. We won the title, GMac was the tournament MVP, and we went on to the NCAA tournament.

After the season, our focus shifted to our incoming freshmen who were still in high school. Our job now was to make sure they were on path to graduate and qualify. My trips to Baltimore were happening weekly. Donte started feeling his stardom, and was slacking academically. There was a chance he was not going to qualify, and I couldn't allow that. Fortunately for all of us, Beverly McNitire at Towson Catholic, helped me monitor Donte's situation from afar and was integral in helping him get his grades up. Donte's family was very helpful as well. Grandma Scott and Uncle Daryl always did whatever it took to keep Donte on a straight path.

Hop's flights and drives to Philly were equally important. Rick and Scoop put themselves in similar situations as Donte, but they pulled through as well. Jonny was the philosopher of the class. He was a qualifier as a junior, so we didn't have to worry about him. We knew we had something special with these incoming freshmen paired with the experience of Devendorf, AO, Paul Harris, and KO.

This freshman class brought some major personalities. Donte was the team jokester! Jonny was the political governor, Scoop was the hustler, and Rick was the methodical uncle. They were all eager to get to the NBA as quickly as they could. But Eric and Paul had those same plans, and were not going to allow the freshmen to come in and take their shine.

The school year began that September with more excitement than ever before. The entire campus was buzzing about our returning players and our talented newcomers lead by Donte and Jonny. Superstar Carmelo Anthony, who led the team to the 2003 national championship, was also on campus to meet with Athletic Director Daryl Gross to solidify plans for the new state-of-the-art basketball facility, the Melo Center, which would soon be under construction. Daryl raised lots of money and gave every athletic facility a facelift upon his arrival in 2004. Daryl was a great leader and great to work with during my tenure at Cuse. Melo, Hakim Warrick, Terrence Roberts, Josh Pace, and a few other former players were all in town the same week.

The open gym runs that week were next level. I saw right away we had the potential to be unstoppable. Our individual skill instruction went well the first few weeks and there was so much competition at every position. It was the most anticipation I felt since I stepped on campus in 2004. Donte was being compared to Melo because he was a skilled combo forward, from the same area of Baltimore and attended the same high school. Jonny was slated to be the next Sherman Douglas, and Paul and Eric were both candidates for the draft following the season. We were on our way, if we could somehow manage all of these egos. Convincing the players to put the team ahead of their individual goals was our mission.

On September 24, 2007, I got the call after workouts that TeNesha's water broke. I ran out of the gym mid-workouts like there was a fire as I dashed to pick her up. Robert Murphy II (RJ) was ready to make his way into the world. As we entered the Crouse hospital and into the delivery room, TeNesha was in a lot of pain. I tried my hardest to joke with her and make her smile to take her mind off things. That didn't go over so well when the pain wouldn't let up.

After getting to the room and situated for delivery, the pain became unbearable, so TeNesha asked the nurse for an epidural. The memory of the needle going into TeNesha's lower back as I held her hand was the scariest thing I had ever seen. TeNesha didn't want to have a C-section, so getting an epidural had to be a part of the birthing process, and now we were ready to push. I had my video camera ready for the action. As the process started, RJ acted like he didn't want to come out. Then all of a sudden, I saw some hair pushing through… One, Two, Three, Push… One, Two, Three, Push! I jumped in with the count to motivate TeNesha. "You got this babe, be strong, T, you got it…" A few minutes later, out popped RJ's head, then his shoulders, and before I knew it, on September 25, 2007 at 3:36 p.m., RJ arrived with a smile on his face, and did not let out a single cry. We knew right away he would be special! We were so excited and very blessed to have a healthy baby boy. I hope my mom was somewhere in the heavens witnessing it all. Watching my wife give birth gave me a whole different appreciation for the strength of a woman. Nothing would be the same after that moment.

Once we were settled at home from the hospital, I jumped right back into workouts on September 27, 2007 with an urgency and focus. Having your first child will motivate you in ways you can't imagine, and for me, it lit a fire that I unleashed in practice on the court. When I got back to work, I had the idea that we should kick start the season with a Midnight Madness event. Midnight Madness is a fun event that marks the start of the college basketball season. It gives fans an opportunity to see the team they'll be watching all season long. Typically, the players are introduced, and then the Head Coach makes a few remarks followed by interactive games with fans, a dunk contest, 3-point shooting contest, and an intra-squad scrimmage.

I knew that Boeheim would care less about this type of event, so he wouldn't be the one I needed to convince. Instead, I met with his wife, Juli, to get her on board. I knew if I could talk her into the idea, she would be able to encourage Coach Boeheim to support it. And that's exactly how it happened. Juli and I finally agreed with administration and marketing on a date for Midnight Madness, and it would be our first in twenty years! I'm always brainstorming how to impact or enhance every program I'm affiliated with. Midnight Madness was good for our players but more importantly, great for the fans and community!

Now that football season was over, fans were eager for the start of Syracuse basketball. Manley had a packed house, and the atmosphere was electric. The crowd was in for a treat. One by one, the players were introduced to the community and Syracuse basketball was once again on the rise! The class of 2007 would turn out to be huge in a number of ways. The three point and dunk contest excited the crowd but the highlight of the evening came during our inter-squad scrimmage when AO shattered the glass with a Darryl Dawkins, tomahawk monster slam dunk! "Broken glass everywhere" (Grand Master Flash voice) which end the festivities. Midnight Madness ended up being a great recruiting weekend for us as we had Tobias Harris, Kris Joseph, and James Southerland in town for the festivities. Ultimately, we ended up signing two out of three of those guys, Kris and James.

At practice, the competition started to heat up. Guys were pushing and clawing to prove their worth. With so much talent and only a few spots, guys knew they had to fight like hell to be in the top 8-player rotation. Depending on the flow of the game, on some nights, Coach employed a 7-man rotation. The Wright/Flynn matchup became the most intriguing to watch. Josh, who was a junior, felt it was his time to take over the point guard duties and lead the program. But Flynn had other plans. They battled daily, but Josh couldn't figure out how to be consistent, and with the pressure mounting, his productivity continued to decrease. Eric had earned his stripes along with Arinze and Paul, so there was only one remaining spot left up for grabs, even though it should have been a no-brainer.

As talented as Donte was, he struggled to pick up the zone principles, and had ZERO interest in playing defense. But because he was a talented McDonald's All-American, and from Baltimore, we had no choice but to make him a starter. Baltimore and Washington, D.C. are two very important cities where we frequently recruit, so it was critical that players coming from these areas were showcased, so that the next talented crop of players from those areas would stay interested in coming to Syracuse. It's no surprise we landed Donte after he saw how Carmelo Anthony's career took off. But Coach Boeheim was not impressed with Donte's motor and was frustrated with his early performance.

"If I had any fucking guts, I would start Kristoff at that spot. He's out-played Donte during most practices," Coach Boeheim would tell me.

I understood Boeheim's thoughts but that would not have worked. We both understood that Donte was the better player so it's was my job to keep pushing him to perform better. In addition, the possible backlash that could happen if Boeheim had Donte coming off the bench could turn tragic. And so, Donte got the starting nod, and to no surprise, he ended up playing extremely well. He settled in, and we started off the season with a bang.

Prior to our first game every NBA organization had visited campus to evaluate our players during practices. I knew we had special talent on our roster when the Vice President of Nike, Nico Harrison and Tim Fuller joined my family and friends at my home for dinner and games during opening weekend of the season. Jonny, Eric, Paul, Donte, and AO were great together. Game one that season was a nail biter! We were in dogfight against Siena. Back and forth we went. I could see how being young may have caught up with us early, but our guys were competing at a very high level. Early in the second half Jonny stole the ball and was going in for a layup, and all of the sudden threw the ball off the back board.... Paul (and his Kaepernick afro) came out of nowhere with a monster slam! The crowd exploded! Coach didn't prefer the showtime antics but it was a joy to see our team having so much fun. With the score tied and twenty-three seconds left on the clock, we called timeout. Coach Boeheim drew up a play for Eric to come off a down screen on the right side, and take the game winning shot. Eric came off the screen open for the shot, but Jonny had other plans. Instead, he took a top of the key 3-pointer and SWISH! The crowd went wild as we won the game! In that moment, I will never forget the look on Eric's face when he got a small taste of what would soon be the Jonny Flynn show.

Chapter Ten
ALL IN

In college basketball, the job of the assistant coaches and support staff is to oversee the day-to-day activities of all the players. This means making sure they attend class, knowing who's in their personal lives, and finding out any pertinent information that could deter them from performing their best academically, during practice and games. The most elite assistant coaches have great relationships with their players, are able to anticipate potential issues, and find ways to fix problems before they escalate to become major issues. The Head Coach acts as the President and CEO of the organization, receiving only the most vital information regarding the players, while leaving the assistants to handle everything else.

At Syracuse, Coach Boeheim entrusted his staff to do their jobs without micromanaging them, and after observing his system for seven years, it was clear to me that there was a good reason he was inducted into the Hall of Fame. After all, it was hard to argue with his results. Boeheim coached 100% of the games, 75% of practice, and by the time I arrived at Syracuse, was heavily involved with USA basketball so recruiting in the spring and summer was limited. He depended on us, his assistant coaches to build relationships with the recruits, and make sure when he arrived the deal was ready to be sealed.

Entering my third season at Syracuse, I had a feeling that we would need to be a lot more hands on. It was undeniable that the 2007 class, led by McDonald All-Americans, Donte Greene and Jonny Flynn, was special. The mark they made on the floor was consistent each game, but it was impossible to overlook Devendorf's talent. Although Jonny hit the game winning shot to start the season, Eric established himself as the leading scorer and was our toughest and most experienced player. Averaging seventeen points and four assists a game during the first nine games, Eric was having the best season of his career until the unthinkable happened. During our game against East Tennessee, Eric tore his ACL and was sidelined for the remaining twenty-five games of the season. This was a huge loss and setback for the team and Eric's career. The freshmen were talented enough to help the team overcome the immediate loss of Devendorf, but none of the new guys had experience competing against the rough and rugged teams in the Big East conference. The lack of veteran leadership turned out to be our downfall.

Once we started league play, our performance fluctuated, which was not a surprise given the fact that we now had to rely solely on our younger players. We started out with two wins at home but once we hit the road it became extremely tough very quickly. We finished overall in ninth place in the Big East, then lost to Villanova in the first round of the Big East tournament. The loss to Villanova kept us out of the NCAA tournament, and we ended up getting invited to the NIT. At Kent State and other mid-major programs, competing in the NIT would be considered a great accomplishment. But at an elite school like Syracuse, it was a slap in the face. To our players, participating in the NIT meant we were "not invited" to the real tournament. We opened to NIT with two wins at home vs Robert Morris and Maryland before losing in the Quarterfinals to a talented UMass team, the second time this season.

The competitor in me HATED to lose that game against UMass, but with the season finally over, a slight weight was lifted off of my shoulders. While preparing my opponent scouts, coaching in practice, future recruiting, being a good husband helping with our new bundle of joy, RJ, it was my job to keep Donte focused all season, which was NOT easy. With his name sitting in the top ten of every NBA mock draft, it was hard for him not to think about going to the next level. Throughout the year, agents kept approaching him from all angles with unbelievable offers of money, cars, etcetera. I had to constantly reiterate the fact that he could not allow the temptation of receiving extra benefits to jeopardize his eligibility and our program's reputation. Constantly having to convince an eighteen year old not to accept cash and cars became exhausting. But Coach Boeheim trusted me to do my job, and I was not going to let him down.

Given the resistance Donte tried to put up, I wasn't surprised when he told me he planned on leaving school to enter the NBA Draft. His mind was made up and there was nothing that would change it; that is, until he met his match in Coach Boeheim. I'll never forget the day Donte went in for his exit meeting after the season to speak with Coach. Donte's plan was to walk into Boeheim's office and TELL him he was leaving. It was a done deal. But when Donte walked back into my office, he sheepishly announced a change of plans. The genius of Syracuse had done it again. Over time, I learned that Boeheim is the master at persuading a player into doing what he wants them to do, and his record speaks for itself.

"Yeah, I think I'm just gonna come back next season, Murph," Donte said.

"What's wrong, what happened in there?" I asked.

"Coach told me I wasn't ready for the NBA. I'm too skinny, my shooting percentages were low, I needed to become a better rebounder, and if I entered the draft, I would probably go in the second round or be undrafted. He made me feel like I ain't shit!"

Coach Boeheim had Jedi mind-tricked Donte into coming back for another season; at least temporarily. I spent the next few days consoling Donte after Boeheim's dissection. Donte then went to speak with his family in Baltimore, and they had other plans in mind. With their blessing, Donte disregarded Coach's assessment and entered the draft anyway. Although Donte seriously considered coming back to Syracuse for another season, who could blame him for leaving (given the draft projections, responsibility he felt to help his family and his girlfriend being pregnant)? Besides, he had originally committed to Syracuse to follow in the footsteps of Carmelo Anthony, who was a lottery pick after playing one season at Syracuse, and embodied the "one and done" era of college basketball.

Coach Boeheim had hoped Donte would take his advice and return for his sophomore year, but wasn't surprised when he announced he was leaving. Donte went on to become a first round pick in the 2008 NBA draft. He always had a great attitude, phenomenal personality, and would give anyone his last penny if they needed it. So, even though he was leaving us, I knew that this would not be the last time I saw Donte. Time would eventually prove that I would never be able to get rid of my forever little big brother. Donte was picked in the first round of the NBA draft by the Memphis Grizzlies, who immediately traded him to the Houston Rockets. A month later Donte was traded again to the Sacramento Kings.

Two weeks after the draft, I received a call from Gersson Rosas, who was then the Director of Player Development for the Houston Rockets.

"Rob, do you have any interest in coaching at the NBA level? Our player development position just opened."

"I do have an interest, Gers, and would definitely love to hear more about it," I replied.

"Sounds good, Rob. We like to do things the right way, so I would like to bring Boeheim in the loop if we're gonna move forward," Gersson said.

"I'll let Coach know what's happening, Gers. Let's talk tomorrow."

A week later, I flew to Houston for my first ever NBA interview for the player development job on Rick Adelman's coaching staff. It was a very different process. During the interview, I was questioned by Gersson, Daryl Morey, and Sam Hinkie from the front office, along with the entire basketball staff. After we met for forty-five minutes, I took some former college players through a forty-minute skill instruction workout to show my on-court abilities. The interview went well, although Coach Adelman himself did not ask me one question. They were considering me and one other candidate, but there was one skill they needed that I could not provide. I had no experience with editing video. Brett Gunning, who was then an assistant from Villanova, ended up getting the job, and is still on the Rockets coaching staff today. Although I was disappointed, I could hear Dr. Tom Clinton (Syracuse Team Psychologist) famous line rang in my head, "sometimes it's good to have high hopes but not high expectations". Doc was always ahead of the curve and gave great advice during our conversations. This interview taught me I should have been more prepared for the opportunity. Ultimately GOD was not ready for my tenure with the Orange to end.

One of the major techniques I learned from Jim Boeheim's coaching style is the importance of giving players the freedom to grow at their own pace, both on and off the court. He is a firm believer in letting players play through their mistakes, and learning life lessons through experience. The beauty of allowing players to figure things out on the court is it lets them get into a rhythm without having the fear that they will be taken out the game if they make one mistake. It also creates an environment of comfort, which leads to the best possible performance. This method has worked for the past forty years in his program.

A downside to this is that players can take on an attitude of invincibleness, and in a small town like Syracuse, the players are already put on a pedestal with fame that is on par with an actual NBA player. Fans would stop them everywhere they went to ask for autographs and pictures, women would swoon over them, and the townies adored the Orange. All of the adulation made it very hard for some players to resist making bad decisions. Away from the court, Coach Boeheim had an expectation that his players will use good judgement in social situations, and represent themselves and the program with class. He is not the type of coach to police the players or keep restating what should be obvious, but it is not always apparent to eighteen, nineteen, and twenty year old men who may be living away from home for the first time. This makes it very easy for guys to get caught up or tempted to take advantage of situations because they don't feel a constant reminder or threat of severe consequences. Poor decisions can lead to a world of problems with women, drugs, and academics on any college campus.

I was an eighteen year old Syracuse University basketball player in my freshmen year. It was little after 10:00 p.m. on a random Friday night when I walked into my apartment full of my rowdy teammates making drinks. This was supposed to be our last wild night out for a while before the season started. I threw my backpack on the floor, and led the team in a round of shots. After a few more drinks, we headed to the Marshall Street bars. A long line of college students draped the front of our favorite bar, Hurry's. We caught everyone's attention as we walked up past the line straight to the front door.

"Good luck this season man!," "OMG, can we take a quick photo with you?," "Go Cuse!," "Is that the basketball team?," "Who's the one that said hi to you in the dining hall?," "OMG, he's so freaking hot!," "My roommate thinks you're hot!"

When we got to the front, security stopped the line and directed us in. A stairwell to the right led down into the infamous bar. All eyes were on my teammates and I as we made our way to the table where the waiter immediately made serving us a priority. We were treated like celebrities everywhere we went. And so, the party began. Drink after drink, song after song, dance after dance, more drinks, and we were off to a good night.

Once the bar was full to capacity, there was this girl who insisted upon getting our attention. She was exciting, bold, and free. You almost couldn't help but be drawn to her confidence. Her blonde hair swung from side to side as she grabbed me from my seat and onto the dance floor. There was a look in her eyes that was inviting, and when she grabbed my arm to pull my ear down to her mouth, her intention was clear.

That night when we left the bar, she insisted on leaving with us. While we all drunkenly stumbled out of Harry's, the girl continued her flirtation with me and my teammates. Who did she come here with? Where were her friends? What dorm does she live in? How many drinks did she have? These are all questions that would have popped into the head of someone in their right mind. But none of us were. We were all drunk.

Eventually, one of my teammates and I headed back to our South campus apartment, and the girl came with us. It was about 3:00 a.m. when the girl started taking her top off so we could have a better look. Her teasing continued when she let her skirt hit the floor. Without words, her body language signaled very clearly what we all thought was a green light to have sex with her. In the heat of the moment, one by one we acted. The two of us took turns having sex with her.

By sunrise, we were fast asleep, sprawled around the apartment. When I opened my eyes, the heaviest hangover set into my forehead. I sat up on my couch and saw my teammate knocked out on the floor. My memory of exactly what happened the night before was a little foggy, but suddenly bits and pieces of the evening popped into my head. Wait! The girl was gone, there was no sign of her anywhere.

An uneasy feeling crept into my stomach, so I immediately woke my teammate up to recap the night. At this point in our college career, we were used to women throwing themselves at us, but had never experienced anything like this. I mean, what a night! But who was that girl? Neither of us was sure we'd even recognize her face if we ever saw it again. Little did we know that it wouldn't be long before her face became one that we'd never forget. A couple of days later, we were both charged with sexual assault of a female student on campus. The months to follow would consist of an ongoing criminal investigation.

This story is an example of how easy it is for athletes to find themselves in situations that can lead to very serious ramifications not only with the school, but with the law. One irresponsible decision can ruin your entire life. It is so important for college athletes to be aware that these sorts of things really do happen, and you will be held accountable if you are involved. There were many variables in this case that all played roles in the outcome. Alcohol was a major factor in the events that led up to this moment. Because alcohol has the ability to impair judgement and affect communication, it is so important that if you're choosing to drink, you are not putting yourself in threatening circumstances.

When it comes to having sex, you have to make sure the other person has given their consent. In this case, the lines blurred when it came to effectively communicating and interpreting consent. If a woman says "no" at any point, whether it seems uncertain or not, take the word literally and stop to avoid any discrepancy. Secondly, if there is any uncertainty about whether someone is incapacitated, don't have sex. In other words, if you are attempting to have sex with a person who is unable to speak coherently, confused on basic facts, can't walk, or is passed out, leave them alone. You are responsible for ensuring consent is clear, voluntary, and unambiguous.

Whether it's was underage drinking, arguments with girlfriends, failing drug tests, or academic issues, there's never a dull moment in college basketball. Things like this happen consistently around the country. Bringing awareness and being in the know is important.

After our players were absolved of wrongdoing, I realized even more the role and responsibility I had as the only black assistant coach on our staff. Having been a former player who had my fair share of girls, and growing up in the hood, I completely understood the culture shock they were going through now that they reached a college campus. A lot of our players were not properly prepared to handle the freedom and trappings of being a high-profile athlete. It was time for me to step up, and make my voice heard. I was there not just to help the team win, but to make an impact in the lives of the young black men who got an opportunity to do more than they were expected to do. Using my relatability and leadership, I needed to start working on their mindsets collectively which would translate in all aspects of life. Improvement on the court, accountability in the classroom, and better interactions and communication with everyone in our program along with other students in the dining hall and campus parties.

The only obstacle to this idea was the mindset of the other coaches. I learned early on at Syracuse, the coaches were territorial about maintaining strong relationships with each kid they recruited. In other words, if Hop recruited a kid, that was "his" kid, and he was supposed to be the one who had the deepest and strongest relationship with him, even if I had more in common with the player. If you were not the lead recruiter of a kid, you were expected to defer to the coach who was and focus on developing a stronger relationship only with "your" players. This philosophy had been in place long before I arrived at Syracuse, and it was clear that things were not about to change. This underlying and unspoken rule sometimes caused resentment among the players as well as the staff, but I learned to keep it moving.

With the sting of not getting the job with the Rockets well behind me, I was looking forward to the start of next season. We had already signed promising forward, Kris Joseph, from Montreal/Washington D.C. and things were looking good for the Orange. Through the coaching pipeline, I ended up hearing about a talented player looking to transfer from Iowa State who was considering a few Big East programs. His name was Wesley Johnson.

As a freshman, Wes averaged 12.3 points and 7.9 rebounds, and was considered the second-best freshman in the Big 12 Conference, but his relationship with his coaches deteriorated his sophomore season, once his left foot started to bother him. Because his foot was swollen from being so active, initial X-rays didn't show anything was wrong, so when he wasn't able to play, the coaches deemed him soft. After a loss, Head Coach Greg McDermott screamed at Wes for sitting out, so he ended up playing through his pain and finished the season averaging 12 points and 4 rebounds. When his older brother Carroll took him to see a different doctor, it was later discovered that Wes wasn't "soft." He actually had a broken foot and proved otherwise by finishing the season despite the pain. Wes's foot was so swollen with interior bleeding the facture did not show up during the

X-rays taken during the season.

I reached out to Oronde, now was an assistant at Oklahoma, who had coached against Wes in the Big 12 conference.

"If you can get him, you should get him," Oronde said. "I know you guys don't take transfers, but if you can get this kid, he's good. He'll fit perfectly at Syracuse."

I had Oronde send me some video of Wes, and I showed the video to Coach Boeheim. Wes didn't make many shots in the video, but I recognized how well he came off the screens. The lift on his jump shot stood out most, and how he hustled for rebounds. Once again, my instinct told me that we HAD to have him, but convincing Coach would not be easy.

"Anytime somebody's transferring," Boeheim said earlier that season, "there's usually a problem."

Coach's philosophy about taking transfer students was very simple: they're usually not worth the risk. In his first thirty years as the head of Syracuse men's basketball, he'd only accepted four transfers. He was doubtful about taking Wes until he ran into the head coach of Iowa State, Coach McDermott, at a Nike event and asked about Wes. Coach McDermott had only good things to say about him. It was only then that Boeheim returned to Syracuse and gave me the green light to go after Wes, but I had actually never stopped recruiting him. I had already put feelers out to several mutual acquaintances we had in the Detroit area. I called his brother and asked if we could set up a visit, and they agreed.

Getting Wes to commit would not be easy. When he first thought about transferring, Arkansas and UConn were his first two choices, while Syracuse wasn't even in the running.

Mike Waters of the Syracuse Post Standard wrote:

Wes Johnson arrived on the Syracuse University campus for his official recruiting visit on Saturday, June 21, 2008.

Johnson, who had decided to transfer out of Iowa State, had flown in from Texas. His older brother, Craig Carroll, had driven from his home in Michigan.

Johnson and Syracuse assistant coach, Rob Murphy, were waiting for him when he pulled up to the Sheraton Syracuse University Hotel & Conference Center.

Over the next two days, Johnson and his brother toured the Syracuse campus. They met Syracuse coach, Jim Boeheim. They saw Manley Field House and the future site of the Carmelo K. Anthony Basketball Center.

"We kept looking at each other and smiling," Carroll said.

Then Murphy took them to the Carrier Dome.

"Wow," Johnson muttered under his breath.

At the end of the official visit, Murphy wanted to get a commitment out of Johnson, but he and his brother hedged. There were planned visits to Pittsburgh and Ohio State, and they were trying to schedule a visit to West Virginia.

Murphy took a chance. He laid out the future.

"He said 'Okay, if you guys want to waste time, go ahead, but I'm telling you in the next couple days, you'll call me back and say, I'm going to Syracuse,'" Murphy said, recalling the final conversation of the trip. "'You're not going to find any place like this. We've got everything you want. You want to be a professional. You'll work hard and play against Paul Harris and all these guys next year in practice, and then next year, you'll probably start for us, we'll have a good year and you'll go pro. It's just that simple.'

"'But you call and let me know, no worries,'" Murphy said, finishing his speech. And they started laughing.

Two days later, Johnson called Murphy.

"I'm coming to Syracuse," he said.

"Coach puts guys like you in a position to be successful," I said. "Our forwards always do well here. Carmelo, Hakim Warrick, Donte Greene, Billy Owens, John Wallace, Derrick Coleman and several others. If you do what you're supposed to do, you'll be a pro."

Throughout the visit, Boeheim not only impressed Wes and his older brother Craig with his knowledge, he showed me an important aspect of recruiting as well. Though we wanted Wes to commit, Coach wasn't pushy or overbearing. He wasn't trying to sell them, he was simply straight forward, which worked. Wes was the first recruit to ever visit Coach Boeheim's home during a visit. I felt the need to do something different to win them over. I believed it would help, but more importantly, I started something new as every assistant started inviting recruits to Coach's house during official visits (trend setter) from that point forward. Before they departed campus, I advised Wes that there was no reason he needed to visit any other schools, because Syracuse was the best situation for him. But supremely confident on what we had to offer, Boeheim instead encouraged Wes and his brother to take other visits, and in just two days after Wes visited, he called with the good news! He was going to be an Orangemen.

When looking ahead to our roster, I felt very good about the upcoming season. I was confident that Kris would make an immediate impact and compliment Eric, Andy Rautins, Jonny, and Paul. Scoop, Rick, and Trishe had worked extremely hard in the off-season, and Arinze was ready to make his mark on the program as well.

Very early in the school year, it was evident that Jonny would have the opportunity to turn pro. Knowing this and after watching me help Donte, he chose to approach me about helping him through the process. I didn't want any tension, so I did my best not to advise Jonny about anything relating to his professional career.

We had a high level of focus to start the season. We were ready to put the previous NIT season behind us, and it showed as we got off to a great start defeating Florida, Kansas, Virginia and Memphis early in non-conference play. Once Big East play began, we realized we had the best backcourt in the conference. Jonny, Eric, and Paul led us all season long and into the Big East Tourney. The most memorable game was when we made history playing and winning the six-overtime game in Madison Square Garden against UConn. It was an instant classic and arguably the most memorable game I've ever coached. After we ran out of gas in the championship game against Louisville we were ready to regroup and make a Final Four run. We started the NCAA tourney with a bang, defeating Stephen F Austin and Arizona State, led by James Harden. We eventually fell to Oklahoma, who was led by Blake Griffin in the Sweet 16. Blake's domination, combined with a bad shooting night for us, ended our great season. This would be the last college game for Eric, Jonny, and Paul but we were very thankful they led us to a twenty eight win season with a Sweet 16 appearance.

LeBron James' agent at CAA, Rich Paul, was determined to sign Jonny as the season closed. Though Jonny was uncertain at first, a visit to Cleveland and LeBron's house sealed the deal. Similar to Donte Greene, Jonny had difficulty deciding whether or not it was the right time for him to go pro or wait until the following year. However, it was undeniable after the season the time was right. In the end, Jonny leaned on his family support system to guide him through the draft process instead of Hop. Our walk-on, Jake Presutti told Hop an inaccurate story (from ear hustling conversations) about myself, Rich, Jonny and Nike which made Hop think that I told Jonny not to consult with him and was leading Jonny's process which was DEFINITELY not the case. I had nothing to do with Jonny's decisions or process whatsoever. This unfortunate misunderstanding caused a rift between Hop and I, making it hard for Hop to trust me in these situations moving forward. Hop's thoughts were a myth in his brain but once he was fixated on a thought it was no changing his mind.

Jonny leaving school to enter the NBA draft was a spot-on decision. He was mature enough, was supported by a great family, and his game was ready. In the 2009 NBA Draft, Jonny was selected with the number four pick overall. Losing Jonny, Eric, and Paul brought some concern to the staff. However, when I asked Boeheim if we should push to keep Eric one more year, he said NO without hesitation. "We'll be better next year without those guys," Boeheim said. I left his office confused on how that would be even close to possible. A Sweet 16 team losing their three leading scorers that won twenty eight games… but as the summer began, I started to understand Boeheim's thought process when I got a visual of the new team. We had a competitive backcourt lead by Scoop, Rautins and Trishe, and a developing group of forwards, Wes, Rick, Joseph, and Sutherland, with two centers led by AO, the loan senior, and DaShonte Riley.

There's always a defining moment when friends become family. We were in the process of building our second home in Syracuse, 6162 Springdale Circle. After selling our home in Camillus quicker than anticipated, we moved everything into storage over a weekend and TeNesha, RJ and I checked into the Residence Inn hotel. Monday afternoon Coach Boeheim walked into my office "Rob, I heard you guys checked into a hotel last night, you're more than welcome to stay at our home until your house is finished being built." Thanks for the offer Coach, but no thanks" I replied.

The following day Coach came back into my office around the same time "Rob, Juli and TeNesha spoke last night, check out of the hotel and be at our house tonight for dinner. You guys will be staying with us until your house is ready". I guess I had no choice, so I called TeNesha to let her know what Coach directed me to do, so we packed up the hotel that evening and we were on Tiffany Circle receiving the security codes to the Taj Mahal, while eating dinner. They allowed us to reside in the basement suite for the next three months. We had everything we needed, and my favorite place was the game room, where I wore out my childhood arcade game, Robotron 2084 most nights. We were extremely thankful for the Boeheim's gesture and something I'll never forget.

It was time to get back on the July recruiting trail. The first stop Coach Boeheim and I made was in Cleveland, OH, to check out our Orange commits CJ Fair and Dion Waiters. They were participating in the Nike, King City Classic. In between games, Coach Boeheim, Hop and me met up with Coach Krzyzewski, Chris Collins and Steve Wojciechowski at the Winking Lizard, downtown 9th Street, for lunch. The aura of Coach K was felt the second we sat down, my first ever lunch with the paragon. The topic of the next hour was constructing the 2010 USA World Championship team. I enjoyed listening and learning the thoughts that went into building the upcoming World Championship team. Most members from the Olympic Gold Medal (Redeem Team), from 2008, would not be participating.

"Lamar (Odom) would be good for this team because of his versatility. Being able to guard 1 through 5 would help us" Said Coach K. Everyone was in agreement, but I remember thinking to myself that Odom was the same player who gave up an offensive rebound to Shawn Marion which led to a 3pt make by Tim Thomas late in the game. That cost the Lakers the first round playoff series against the Suns in 2006. I'm a die-hard Laker.

"I'm concerned about Rondo with this group. He's an introvert and doesn't talk much to his teammates. He's a leader but in his own way, I'm not sure if he will be good for this team" Boeheim mentioned. "I believe we need as many versatile players that can play both ends on the floor effectively, like Kevin (Durant), Andre (Iguodala), Rudy (Gay), and I love Russell, he gets after it every possession. He'll find his way on the team" Said Coach K. I was working for a Hall of Famer in Coach Boeheim, but at the completion of this lunch, I had a clear understanding of why Coach K is the big boy that the big boys watch in the coaching profession. The ultimate leader! Undoubtedly, the best basketball lunch I ever experienced, and I was very excited about watching the upcoming Olympic team practices in Vegas later in the month.

That fall, I was back in Detroit recruiting, and stopped by a recording studio to see Murray. He was producing music with Denotes, Mae Day and a few other rap and R&B artists. We had a huge basketball debate which included LeBron James who I've been an advocate of for almost twenty years. The artist eventually challenged me to go into the booth and freestyle. I accepted the challenge.

"Ball team come through, we shut it down, man ya already knew we shut it down, Syracuse what we do, we shut it down, shut it down —— Let's go Murph's back, Murph rap, ya'll already know where Murph at, we every-where, you ain't never there, you seen us shutting down Madison Square (The Garden).... This is how you get the crowd pop'n, dance team, cheerleaders, RJ's rock'n —— Ball team come through, we shut it down, man you already knew, we shut it down!"

Needless to say, I rocked the mic. I put a couple of verses together about our upcoming team and season off the top of my head, and surprisingly it came out really good. About a month later, as I was driving AO to class, I played the CD with my freestyle. He enjoyed it so much that he asked me if he could play it in the locker room for his teammates. Obviously, the players went crazy when they heard it!

A few weeks later, "Shut It Down" was introduced at Midnight Madness and became the team's anthem for the rest of the season. Before I knew it, the slogan, "Shut It Down" had taken on a life of its own. CDs were being sold, T-Shirts were being sold at Manny's, a best seller on iTunes, and the entire Carrier Dome was rocking to my rap song. Once we beat No. 3 North Carolina at Madison Square Garden, the third game of the season on national TV, "Shut It Down" became a national anthem. A few games later, the SU dance team and cheer squad performed a in game routine to the song wearing the shirts and the movement could not be stopped! A percentage of the profits from Shut It Down was donated to the Jim & Juli Boeheim foundation.

Even more importantly, we had the squad that merited the hype. Given extended minutes, Andy came into his own and became a clutch shooter, Scoop was more comfortable in his role, and with the addition of Wes, and the maturation of Kris Joseph we became the #1 team in the country. AO remained a huge part of anchoring our zone, and Brandon Triche became a silent assassin. With these pieces in place, we were excited about the season.

Before our fantastic start to the season, we suffered an embarrassing defeat that grabbed our attention and forced us to get it together very quickly. During our second exhibition game of that season, we lost to Division II Le Moyne College. Trying to prove a point to the players about why we play zone, Coach Boeheim had the team play man-to-man defense the entire game. He proved his point, but the game turned out to be a complete disaster. It goes without saying that Coach would never repeat that decision again, but I felt because of this loss we were more focused than ever. After the game, I remember sitting in our meeting room inside the Carrier Dome, starring at each other until 2am. Of course, this did not help solve anything or change the embarrassment we had to deal with for losing this game.

Fortunately, the loss didn't actually count against our regular season record because it was an exhibition game. We used the humbling experience as motivation, and it ended up helping us have one of the best starts in the school's history. Within a few weeks, we went from being unranked to a top ten team while jamming to "Shut It Down." Our chemistry came together very quickly. Wes was just as good as we advertised, and when the lights went up, he always performed at an optimal level. We got off to a 24-1 start. I was experiencing one of the best seasons I had experienced at Syracuse thus far. Not bad for a team with no McDonald All-American s and no top 50 recruits coming out of high school. Even with the loss of Jonny, Eric, and Paul, we didn't miss a beat, as Coach Boeheim predicted.

The season was going great, the holiday season was in full effect and it could not have been a better time for TeNesha and me to learn we were expected our second child! We were excited for ourselves but more importantly that our son, RJ, would soon have a sibling to bond, play and grow with in the near future.

Also during this time, I was approached about doing a live TV segment on *Rewind and Reload,* which was a weekly show developed to cover Syracuse basketball on the local ABC affiliate, News Channel 9, with Steve Infanti. I always wanted to do television, but I was nervous when they approached me. I

didn't feel prepared to do live TV, but this was the #1 station in the market. I knew that I couldn't pass up this opportunity, so I began to practice by speaking to myself in the mirror. I also sat in a few communication classes, taught by Dr. Wright, at the renowned Newhouse school of Communication.

A week later, we went live and after two shows, I was hired to be a part of the show for the remainder of the season. I was happy to be brought back to the show for a second season the following year. It was a tremendous development experience for me.

Even though the opportunity was initially intimidating to me, I have always known that television was something I would like to do after my coaching career. Over the years, I have watched Kenny Smith, Jalen Rose, Stephen A. Smith, and Shannon Sharpe, among others, all do an amazing job of representing sports and their opinions on television. They have all carved out a successful niche in both educating and entertaining the public. I am thankful to Steve Infanti and all the folks at New Channel 9, who gave me this opportunity, as it not only prepared me to become a head coach, it also helped me prepare for a career after coaching.

We roared into the NCAA Tournament with a record of 28-3, but were dealt a devastating blow during the quarterfinals of the Big East tournament when Arinze got hurt against Georgetown. Even though we were still awarded a No. 1 seed, we ended up losing to a good Butler team in the Sweet 16 in Utah. Had Arinze not gotten hurt, I believe we would have won the national championship. He meant that much to our zone defense. It was sad to see AO get hurt his senior season as he was having the best year of his college career, and we were on our way to the Final Four. I truly wished for AO to have the Final Four experience before he graduated Syracuse, but God had other plans.

After the crushing loss, I knew Wes would decide to go pro. We had a great year overall, and Wes was projected to be a top five pick in the 2010 NBA Draft. Just as I predicted, he went on to be drafted by the Minnesota Timberwolves, with the number four pick that year. Wow, I mean what a feeling! To be able to directly impact that level of a change in someone's life feels great. I was so incredibly proud of Wes and the journey he trusted me to lead him on.

It's inevitable in the recruitment process that you build a bond. I always looked at my recruits as if they were my actual family. In fact, Wes and Kris were called the "Murphy boys" all season, and were truly like sons to me. The bond we formed was about more than just basketball. Even after a player's college career was finished, I intended to always be someone that a player could call on. Today, Wes is one of the few players from Syracuse, who is still playing in the NBA, from my tenure coaching the Orange. It is a great source of pride to know the role I play in helping players I coach blossom, reach and maintain the platform they deserved in their careers. Throughout my life, I've learned that you should help as much as you can for as many people as you can without any expectation of return. That is how I live my life, and the main reason blessings continue to come my way.

A few weeks after Wes was drafted into the NBA, I experienced the greatest high ever for a second time! On July 2, 2010, we were on our way back to Crouse hospital to prepare for the birth of our beautiful baby girl, Ryann Andrea Murphy. I remember vividly packing up and heading to the hospital at 6am once again trying to keep TeNesha strong as the stomach kicks continue during our morning drive. Once we were checked in TeNesha and I joked for hours as the pain came and went all day long. The evening approached and finally Ryann decided she was ready for her birthing process to begin. One, two, three push… One, two, three push… TeNesha knew the drill and before you knew it Ryann popped into our lives like a super nova. There was no plan, but there she was screaming and kicking. Life would never be the same once she arrived. Thoughts of wanting to protect this little girl forever would not leave my mind. I also learned quickly that she would give us a run for our money, and I was not wrong about that! Ryann has been a sassy diva since she was born, and I would not have it any other way. Ryann has also excelled in multiple sports and loves to compete.

Chapter Eleven

BELIEVE IT'S YOURS UNTIL IT'S NOT

T he 2010 – 2011 season after Ryann was born was full of highs and lows. With the loss of Wes and Andy, it was time for Kris Jo, B Trishe, and Scoop Jardine to take over the program. Our incoming freshmen class with Dion Waiters, C.J. Fair, Fab Melo and Baye Moussa Keita proved to be as good as advertised. We were ranked in the top twenty of both polls to begin the season and sky rocketed to a 18-0 start. In the middle of conference play we got hampered with a few injuries and started to struggle. After back-to-back losses to Georgetown at home and Louisville on the road, we started to get concerned. If we wanted to make a final four run, we believed Coach Boeheim needed to have more confidence in Dion and allow him to play more minutes. Dion and Coach Boeheim were like oil and water, and Hop spent all season trying to find ways to gel the relationship. Dion was a stubborn freshman who believed he was the best guard in the program, and there was no denying that because he was. However, Coach Boeheim despised Dion's work ethic and bad attitude.

After the Louisville loss half way through the conference season, the staff met, as we usually did the following day, to review film. Right before we met, Hop came into my office and asked me to speak up about Dion during the meeting. He explained that if he brought up Dion himself, Boeheim wasn't going to listen since he would be taking up for his own recruit. On the other hand, Hop believed that if I said something, Boeheim would look at the situation differently. I believed Dion was our most talented guard and should be playing more, so I told Hop I would say something positive and allude to the fact that we needed Dion on the floor to reach our full potential.

As halftime of the film approached, Coach Boeheim asked, "Does anyone have anything to say about what they've seen so far?" The room stayed quiet until our guru of video, Todd Blumen, went on a rant about how our rebounding is one of the problems. I chimed in shortly after and brought up Dion.

"I think for us to get better, we need to play Dion more minutes," I said.

Coach turned and glared at me, "Dion? He's lazy, he's not coachable, all he cares about is scoring the ball, and both of our starting guards, Brandon and Scoop, work their asses off. Dion needs to start working before he can play more," Boeheim said.

"Coach, I get that, but he's better than those guys. If we can get him to work and allow him to play more, we could be better," I countered.

"I don't wanna hear that shit, Dion is not the reason we just got our asses kicked the last two games. You don't know what the hell you are talking about!" Boeheim yelled.

"Coach, Coach...," I tried to intervene.

"I don't wanna hear shit!" Boehiem said as he cut me off.

"Okay, I won't say nothing then!" I respond.

"Get out, just get the HELL OUT... fuck'n Dion, I don't wanna hear shit about him!" Boeheim remarked.

"Nah, Coach, I'm gonna watch the second half but will keep my mouth closed" I stated.

The room was completely silent as Todd began to roll the film. We got through the second half, and no one made a peep. I tried to get the message across but failed terribly. After we left the meeting, Bernie came to me and said, "Murph, I've been with Jimmy forty years. He's as stubborn as ten mules. I agree that you are right in what you said, but there's a reason why the meetings are always quiet. You've been here seven years; I thought you would've learned that by now."

We ended up finishing the season strong, tied for overall third place in the Big East conference. We fizzled out early in the Big East tourney, which was disappointing. This hurt our chances of getting a top four seed in the NCAA tourney. In most cases, your seed can determine your success in the Big Dance. We dominated the first round against Indiana State, but Marquette was waiting for us in the second round. A Big East rival loaded with toughness and talent had already beat us on their turf earlier in the season. Back and forth we battled, and with 1:22 remaining, Kris Jo gave up a three point shot on the right wing to Jae Crowder, which broke our backs and solidified Marquette's victory. We had a great opportunity to win, but did not deliver down the stretch when it mattered most. We all expected the season to end on a higher note but God had other plans. Ironically Dion led us in scoring with 18 points vs Marquette and sixteen months later, after never starting a single game at Syracuse University, went on to become the number four pick in the NBA draft. No other guard on that roster played a minute in the NBA.

By season's end, a few head coaching jobs came across my desk that piqued my interest. The coaching carousel spins every March in college basketball. Coaches all over the country get fired and hired during this time. The turnover, instability, and lack of job security are all pitfalls that come with coaching at the college level.

I knew that becoming a head coach, especially as an African-American, would be difficult. However, my instinct pushed me to inquire about the job openings. Statistics have shown that the number of African-American coaches is nominal in the big picture. As I mentioned earlier, black coaches are unfairly thought of as only being recruiters and not leaders/coaches, a stigma that has hindered our career advancement for decades. But if I didn't at least try to put myself out there, I knew I would regret it.

Kent State University happened to be one of the head coach openings at this time. Geno Ford, formerly the head coach at Kent, moved on to Bradley University for the same position. Geno and I worked together during my tenure at Kent as an assistant coach, so I was familiar with the program's structure. It would be impeccable timing to take over Kent State, given all the returning talent they had in place for next season, and my prior experience within the program. But in order for me to have a chance, I would have to beat a sure candidate and former colleague, Rob Senderoff, who was still an assistant coach at Kent.

We both knew the program inside out. The only major difference in the two of us was that he was white and currently working at Kent, and I was black and now an assistant coach at Syracuse. I proceeded to go after the job knowing that I should be considered for the position. In the process of figuring out what I could do to increase my value as a candidate, I decided to call Antonio Gates to see if he would help. After all, Antonio was the greatest basketball player to ever wear the Kent State uniform, and led the Flashes to the Elite 8 in the NCAA Tournament. Given our history and relationship, I knew Antonio would do all he could to help me land the position. Once I was in the pool of candidates, I continued to gain support through my contacts, and of course my opponent Rob had done the same.

The last string I pulled was to have Antonio speak with Athletic Director, Joel Nielsen, and promise to donate $400,000 over the next three years to the basketball program if I was hired. At the Final Four in Houston, I had an interview with Joel Nielsen and his Associate Athletic Director, TK. I thought my interview went very well. There was nothing else I could do to position myself further. If the job was for me, I would get the call.

One day passed, then two, and on the third day my agent called and told me they decided to go in a different direction. Just like that, my heart fell to my stomach. I actually cried in my kitchen when I told my wife I didn't get the job. I truly felt this was it; I was supposed to be the head coach at Kent State. I was ready to take over that program. Even with being a current assistant coach there, one of their most famous alumni supporting me with a generous donation to the athletic department, and my experience working for a Hall of Fame coach at Syracuse, there was still one thing that I could not change… I was black. Rob Senderoff went on to become the head coach of Kent State University and deservedly so.

I struck out with Kent State, but God had another plan in store. While at the Final Four in Houston, I spent most of my time networking and hanging out with Tony Harvey, the former Mizzou assistant who recruited Mo Ager while I was the head coach of Crockett High. Ironically, I met T Harv in 1997 when he was an assistant coach at Eastern Michigan University. Early on in my career, T Harv helped me and other young coaches understand the landscape of college basketball.

That weekend, I went to a happy hour gathering where T Harv introduced me to Derrick Gragg, who was then the Athletic Director at Eastern Michigan. I ended up really hitting it off with Derrick and his wife, Sanya. As they departed the restaurant, Sanya looked at me, and then said to Derrick aloud, "This will be your next head basketball coach. You're gonna hire him one day." I laughed it off without thinking too much about what she said. But I thought it was very endearing of her to make such a comment.

After a good Final Four weekend, Monday rolled around and it was time to head back to Syracuse. On my way to the airport, I got wind of a rumor that the head coach of Eastern Michigan was on the brink of getting fired. I said to myself, "No way! I just met the AD and his wife, and they never led me to believe a change was coming." This just had to be a swirling rumor. To my surprise, a few days later the news hit the wire, "Charles Ramsey has been relieved of his duties as the Head Coach of Eastern Michigan University." I immediately received what seemed to be a million calls about my interest in the job, and all I could think about was Sanya saying to Derrick, "This will be your next hire…," as they walked out of the restaurant six days earlier.

> You never know when an opportunity is going to present itself or who is listening. This is why I cannot stress enough how important it is to make a good impression on people you meet and seek genuine relationships. Be very purposeful in how you dress, your body language and how you greet people. Being an active listener and looking people in the eye when you speak to them, will show people that you are engaged in the conversation and that you truly care. These practices will be part of what will allow you stand apart from others and make the right impression.

Although the emotions I went through not landing the Kent State job had finally worn off, I questioned whether or not I wanted to put myself through another potential let down again. But I reasoned why not? I decided to go after the job harder than I did at Kent State. Right away, I had my agent call to see if I could get in the pool to be interviewed. My agent's immediate response was not very optimistic.

"Well, I'm told they have a list of guys in mind already, Rob, so you're gonna probably be on the outside looking in. I'll work on getting you an interview, but it doesn't look good," Jason said.

I was not trying to hear him, and quickly rattled off all of the reasons why I would be the PERFECT candidate.

"I'm a Detroit native, I've won two state championships as a high school coach in the state of Michigan, I've coached in the most successful program in the MAC conference at Kent State, I'm working for Hall of Fame Coach Jim Boeheim at Syracuse University, and I can't get in the candidate pool at Eastern Michigan? Get the heck out of here!"

I was pissed, to say the least. Everyone I spoke with told me there was no way I could get the job. The word on the street was that Eastern was set on hiring a white head coach. They didn't want to hire someone with the same profile of the man they just fired. Coach Ramsey was an African-American assistant coach at Michigan when he was hired to lead the Eagles. The similarities between us were too parallel for them. Eastern was seeking a coach who had not worked this past season, or a former head coach. The top three names rumored to potentially get the job were Todd Lickliter, Tim Buckley, and Dane Fife. Lickliter had past success as a head coach. Buckley was a former head coach in the MAC conference, and was a current assistant at Indiana. Although Fife didn't have much success as a head coach, he was on the great Tom Izzo's staff. Not surprisingly, all three of the front-runners for the job were white.

The president of Eastern Michigan at the time was Sue Martin. She and Coach Ramsey never saw eye-to-eye on anything. Ramsey didn't win many games, but he ran a clean program and graduated all of his student athletes. I was also told that President Martin was not too fond of black folks in general, so it seemed like my agent was right. My chances were slim to none. But my instincts told me not to give up, and I refused to quit trying. I had everyone I knew in the state of Michigan call the AD, and send letters on my behalf. They flooded the EMU athletic office with everything "Rob Murphy," and I still couldn't get an interview. I remember T Harv calling me to explain the real deal.

"Rob, fall back on trying to get the EMU job. Derrick cannot hire you. The board and the President will not allow him to hire another black coach at this time. My sister talks to him every day, and I speak to him every few weeks. It's a funny deal going on up there. They already have a black football coach, a black women's basketball coach, and a black baseball coach. And Derrick is black himself. Believe it or not, unfair or not, they don't like how the athletic department looks right now. It's just too much color, so Derrick must go white for this hire, and for his career. There's no chance… I hate to be this honest, but he specifically told me to tell you to fall back because he doesn't wanna waste your time. He knows if you get placed in the pool it would only be for HR reasons. But you really would have no chance."

I kept very quiet during this call, and all I could think about is what I could do to overcome this. I didn't want to accept it! I hung up the phone and called Oronde, who also had a connection to Dr. Derrick Gragg because of their working relationship at Arkansas. Oronde advised me to stay after the job and not to stop until someone was hired. "Believe it's yours until it's not," he said.

The hiring pool was complete on Saturday, April 9, 2011, and the interviews were scheduled to start the following Monday, April 11. The week prior to the hiring pool being completed, I did everything I could to get in, and finally I got the call that Tuesday. I was in. Getting into the pool alone is sometimes the hardest task for black candidates. At that point, I just had to wait for an interview time. When Thursday morning rolled around, and I still hadn't heard from anyone, I started to get concerned because they said they were set to have a final decision that Saturday.

By nightfall, I figured I probably wasn't going to get a shot. I sat around frustrated all night until my phone finally rang at about 9:00 p.m. It was my agent calling me to say, "Rob, they want to bring you in tomorrow evening, and you'll interview with the President on Saturday morning at 8:00 a.m. before she goes off to graduation."

"Well, what the heck does that mean, Jason?"

"You wanted a chance, and this is the only interview time they could find to bring you in. They probably threw you in the pool for HR purposes just to say they interviewed a black person, to be honest. Everyone has said they are going white, so at least you know what you're dealing with," he explained.

After listening to my agent, I was very discouraged and angry, so I vented to TeNesha.

"I'm pulling my name out of this. My agent just called. He said the AD has already told him I have no chance. So, forget it then, I'm done," I exclaimed.

"Just go, who cares, go for the experience. You never know what can happen. And all those folks who called on your behalf, you're letting them down. Keep using the interviews as experience, if nothing else. It's not gonna hurt anything," TeNesha encouraged.

Every aspect of this process pointed in a negative direction for me. Still, out of respect, I let Coach Boeheim know that I was interested in the job.

"Why that job?" he asked. "You can stay here another year, and get a better job than that. Can you win there?"

Coach Boeheim didn't really like change, so his reaction was slightly biased. Michigan was my home state, and I knew I could get that program going if given the opportunity. Also, it was too ironic that Eastern Michigan was the school I would have attended if I had scored high enough on the ACT back in high school. It could only be fate that would bring me full circle to this university again. I took some time to think about it. After thirty minutes or so, I agreed that TeNesha was right. What would be the harm in just going for the interview? I had already prepared an entire interview booklet to present, and who knew; something from the experience could be beneficial. I set my emotions aside and focused on becoming the next men's basketball coach at Eastern Michigan University.

On Friday evening, I flew to Detroit and checked into the Ypsilanti Marriott Eagle Crest Hotel. This was one good sign, since I'm the Mariano of the Marriott. Once I got settled, I looked over my interview booklet about 100 more times before calling it a night. But right before I fell asleep, something told me to call Coach Boeheim.

"Coach, I know it's midnight, but my interview starts at 8:00 a.m. at the President's house, and I need a little advice."

"No worries Rob, I spoke with the President today, and I thought the conversation went well. She didn't seem to be leaning either way, but my advice would be for you to go in there and say whatever you like. Interview them, as opposed to them interviewing you. Who cares? What's the worst that can happen? You have a great job here at Syracuse, so don't worry about it," he advised.

That brief conversation shifted my entire mood and plans for my interview. I had nothing to lose, and being reminded of that alleviated a ton of pressure.

When I woke the next morning, I was READY! I had Jay-Z's "Already Home" bumping through the speakers at 6:45 a.m. *"Eat food already, ain't nothing given, you gotta claim your shoes already. Yeah, so on this summation I don't know who you racing, I'm already at the finish line with the flag waving."*

The associate AD, Mike Malach, picked me up from the Marriott, and halfway through our ride, I decided to ask Mike if a decision was already made.

"Do I really have a legit opportunity here?" I inquired.

"Well, anything can happen," he said.

I still felt I had no chance when I hopped out of his car for the interview, but it was game time. I proudly walked into the President's office, introduced myself, and immediately took over the conversation. I started with my booklet, "The Perfect Fit," which detailed my plans for the first thirty days, and then the first 100 days being the head coach. I emphasized my recruiting ties throughout the state of Michigan and the country, and I pressed on how I could make an instant impact by turning the entire program around this upcoming season. It was clear that the President felt pressure to find the right person for the job and that this new hire couldn't be a mistake.

"I'm your guy then, anyone else would be a mistake. There is no one better for EMU than me. You will not go wrong, I'm the perfect fit," I confidently stated.

Though the President looked at me as if I grew two heads, I could feel that her perception of me was changing as the interview went on. My confidence, energy, knowledge, and plan for EMU basketball was undeniable. By the end of our meeting she had one small piece of advice for me.

"When you go into the next room with our eight regents, make sure you talk a lot less in there," she said.

I laughed, "Thanks for having me, and I hope I'm your next head coach."

When I walked into the room full of regents, I didn't take her advice. My goal was to interview everyone and let them know MY plan to turn the program around, so I approached the regent group the exact same way.

From start to finish, I commanded the attention of the entire room. In that moment, I was second to none. I then interviewed with EMU basketball Hall of Famer, Earl Higgins and one current player, Derrick Thompson, and I was confident about the impression I left on them.

When I finally got to Derrick Gragg he asked, "What have you said to everyone? I thought you had no chance, but everyone is raving about you!"

"I'm just being myself and sharing my vision for the EMU basketball program," I said.

"Well, share it with me!" Derrick was eager to hear my plans.

After our conversation, he understood why everyone was so impressed, and from there, I knew all eyes were on Rob Murphy. I left that office undoubtedly satisfied with my performance, and when Mike Malach dropped me back off at the hotel, he said, "I don't know what you did, but your name is ringing positively with everyone on campus." I knew I did my very best, so no matter what the outcome was moving forward, I would be okay with their decision.

I flew out to Baltimore the next day to hop back on the recruiting trail for the Orange. I landed at BWI Sunday evening with plans to check out Jerami Grant, Justin Anderson, James Robinson and Kam Williams on Monday. These were my top targets for the 2012 and 2013 classes I was planning to recruit to Syracuse, all playing in the DMV area. As soon as I arrived at the Hertz Rental Car location, my phone rang. The area code read 734.

"Hello…," I answered.

"Hey, Rob, it's Derrick Gragg from Eastern Michigan."

"Hey, what's up Derrick?"

"I know this is gonna shock you, but ummm, I'm very close to offering you our head coaching position here at Eastern Michigan, but need to ask you a few more questions first," he said.

I had a grin from ear to ear on the other end of the phone because I KNEW I had the job, and now the ball was in my court. After talking to Derrick for about twenty-three minutes, he made me the offer to be the next Head Men's Basketball Coach at Eastern Michigan. I told him I was in Baltimore, and wanted to discuss the situation with my family before making a decision.

I arrived home about 5:00 p.m. on Monday, and had already spoken with TeNesha at length the night before. As happy as TeNesha was for me, she was against moving back to Michigan because she never really liked it. She also gained a strong social circle in Syracuse that couldn't compare. In addition to all of this, I previously had the opportunity to leave Syracuse to take a job at the University of Kentucky after my second season with the Orange. Most of TeNesha's family lived in Kentucky, and at that time, we were pregnant with our first child. TeNesha wanted me to take the UK opportunity at that time so she could be closer to most of her family, which could have helped her navigate as a first-time mom. But I turned down that opportunity to stay with Jim Boeheim at Syracuse. Moving back to Michigan meant that we would be moving close to my family and closer to hers which could benefit us all.

I knew that her feelings about Michigan would not stand in the way of the opportunity, but I needed her full support if I was going to take on a head coaching position. After speaking with several people whose opinions meant a lot to me, it became clearer that taking this opportunity was an absolute must. Coach Boeheim, Troy Weaver, Scott Perry, Oronde Taliaferro, Ra Murray, Chris Grier Luchey, Will Smith, and several others had only positive advice and support for me taking on the challenge. This opportunity in many ways mirrored my journey to transform the Crockett High School program. I would be starting from the bottom and building up.

When TeNesha gave it further thought and agreed we couldn't pass it up, there was no turning back. I called Derrick and asked him if I could have one more night to sleep on it. Derrick told me if he did not hear from me by noon the next day, they would move in another direction. He ended up calling me the next morning at 10:11 a.m., asking how I felt. After talking to him for ten minutes, I accepted the job to become the Head Coach of EMU.

On Thursday April 21, 2011, I was introduced as the twenty-ninth Head Coach at Eastern Michigan University. It's a day I will never forget. Having all my friends and family in the crowd during the press conference was truly remarkable. To be able to become a head coach thirty minutes from where I grew up was unbelievable. The press conference and media interviews went perfectly. Without delay, I had my first team meeting and connected with the players. I told the current coaches and support staff I would meet with them the following week to let them know my thoughts and plans.

That evening my family and I went to dinner to celebrate, and then I returned to Syracuse to wrap up my final chapter with the Orange. Wow, I couldn't believe it. I always knew I had what it took, but I was astonished that I was given the opportunity to rebuild and lead a successful Division I basketball program. It quickly became national news that I was leaving Syracuse to be the head coach at Eastern Michigan University.

Saying goodbye to my Syracuse family was more difficult than any other part of my journey to the next phase. The current and incoming players I helped recruit to the program were the toughest to face because while everyone was happy for me, they also didn't want me to leave. Kris Jo, C.J. Fair and family, along with incoming freshman, Rakeem Christmas, and his aunt, Jameela Amira, each had certain expectations of me for the coming summer and following season. I assured them they would be in great hands, and I promised to do all I could for the betterment of their basketball careers from afar.

Before I left, I wanted to solidify a multi-game deal with Syracuse. Every year at Eastern Michigan, I learned that we needed to raise money by playing guaranteed games. Power 5 level programs (ACC, Big Ten, Big East, Big 12, SEC, PAC 12) along with a few mid-major plus programs (AAC, Atlantic 10) pay smaller athletic programs good money to fill their home schedules yearly, so I thought why not go back home and play the Orange? Syracuse is where my career evolved, and the Orange will always be special to me. Coach Boeheim didn't hesitate to help make this happen. The Eastern program was operating on a low budget, and these guaranteed games against Syracuse would be beneficial to both programs.

My very last stop before getting on the road to Michigan was to visit with center, DaShonte Riley. DaShonte was already on the verge of transferring from Syracuse to another school, and was coming off a foot injury. We already had two other centers in the Orange program, and with his poor work ethic at this point, he wasn't going to see much playing time anytime soon.

Prior to me applying for head coaching positions, I was in communication with a few schools to see if they would be interested in DaShonte, but once I took over at EMU, I knew having him in my program could help speed up the building process, and benefit his college basketball career. At Syracuse, he was a role player, but at EMU he was good enough an impact player.

By Monday, I was in Ypsilanti getting prepared to hire my staff. Side note: anyone who receives a head Division I coaching job should immediately change their cell number! My phone rang nonstop with calls and text messages for the next three weeks. Some people wanted to congratulate me, but most people were trying to get any and every job in the program I had to offer. Let's just say, I was presented with more options than I needed.

Obviously before I moved forward with any staffing decisions, I called my famous mentor, Coach Boeheim. He told me my hires wouldn't matter in the big picture, because I was a young head coach. He felt I needed to do most of the recruiting and focus on implementing my system. Whoever I hired needed to be a good listener and coachable. I, on the other hand, originally wanted some "go getters." But I took Boeheim's advice and decided not to hire all recruiters. In that conversation, Boeheim expressed how highly he thought of me, both as a recruiter and a coach, and in that moment, I was reassured that I made the right decision taking on the challenge to build a successful program at EMU.

After meeting with all of the staff members under Coach Ramsey, I let them know that I was moving in a different direction. My first hire was Mike Brown. He was someone I had known for years, and he was hungry to come back home for an opportunity to coach in the Mid-American Conference. Mike was sharp, detail-oriented, and was a very effective coach and recruiter. He understood the Academic Progress Rate forward and backwards, something I knew was important. I'm forever appreciative of Mike; he really helped me lay a solid foundation at Eastern Michigan. His diligent work helps our continued success, even today.

My second hire was Kevin Mondro. Dro was very persistent in pursuing the job, and he proved to me why he should be part of EMU basketball. Throughout his career, he was known to be loyal, and was always the hardest worker on any staff. I had also known Dro for fifteen years, so I was familiar with all he would bring to the table. Dro has been with me for eight years at EMU, and continues to help us improve all aspects of our program year to year. Dro will be a head coach in the near future. I'm very thankful for all he's done to help move the needle at EMU.

My next hire was Benny White. EMU regent, Jim Stapleton, and the Mayor of Detroit, Dave Bing, suggested that I bring him on board. Benny is another person I had known for years. His hire turned out to be helpful in several areas of our program. Benny is a very good coach but his teaching of life to our student-athletes daily had the biggest impact. He always remained positive through all the ups and downs during his tenure.

I then searched the country for the perfect director of basketball operations, but could not come up with the right person. Over dinner one evening, TeNesha had an idea, "Maybe Vic would be good for the job!"

"Vic? Really? You think so?" I questioned.

"Yes!" TeNesha said.

I met Victoria Sun through Troy Weaver at the 2005 Basketball Hall of Fame ceremony when Coach Boeheim was being inducted. Vic is a Syracuse graduate who played on the tennis team, and was a manager for the men's basketball team. Our Syracuse ties spurred us to develop a friendship, and I discovered that Vic too BLEEDS Orange! Throughout my time at Syracuse, we kept in touch, and she was always calling or texting to show support for the team. After graduating, she became a sportswriter, so I wasn't sure if she would be interested.

I took some time to think on it, and realized Vic did fit the mode of everything I was looking for. She's loyal, smart, a hard worker, understands the game of basketball, communicates well, is prompt, and reliable. So, I called Coach Boeheim to get his thoughts.

"Coach, I'm thinking about calling Vic to see if she would been interested in becoming my Director of Basketball Ops. What do you think?"

"I think she'd do a great job. Is she interested?" Boeheim asked.

"I'm not sure, but I wanted your take on it before I reached out," I said.

"Well, I think she would be great, Murph. Let me know what you decide," he said.

Next, I called Troy Weaver.

"Weave, I'm thinking about calling Vic about my Ops position, what do you think?"

He laughed. "Vic? You can't get Vic, she's overqualified, and she is living in California. That would be great if you can get her, Murph."

"Okay, I'm gonna call her today," I replied.

That day I called Vic, and lucky for me, she had an interest. We flew her in a few days later so she could get a feel for the program, campus and area. If she wanted the job, it was hers. After the trip, she said yes, and moved across the country to help us build the EMU basketball program. Vic was by far the most dynamic hire I made to start my tenure at EMU. Whenever something was needed to be taken care of, it was done before I could even ask Vic to handle it. Victoria Sun is the most loyal, supportive, and dedicated woman in our industry I've ever come across. Jake Presutti, Wendale Farrow and Derrick Davis made up our support staff and all did a tremendous job helping lay the Coach Murphy foundation at EMU.

Once the staff was in place, we started our recruiting efforts. We wanted to make recruiting kids in Michigan a priority; therefore, we actively reached out to every high school coach and every top player in the state. I knew we also needed some transfers from high-level schools to assure our future success. I already had DaShonte Riley on board, and I heard that Glenn Bryant, who started his career at Arkansas, was also interested in transferring closer to home. I made a call to Glenn's AAU coach, Carl Weaver, and a visit was set. Glenn was a done deal. Those two transfers, originally from the state, brought instant credibility to Eastern Michigan basketball and both had something to prove.

Things were heating up and we were well on our way, but the high school landscape remained tough to tackle. With the University of Michigan up the street, Michigan State only seventy miles away, rival schools, Central and Western Michigan to compete with, and University of Detroit and Oakland being local, getting the best players from Michigan would be a challenge. One of our first unofficial visits was with Bryn Forbes. Forbes was another player who we believed could quickly change the program. After visiting him on campus, we thought we would get him, but he decided on going to Cleveland State, so we quickly moved on.

Austin Harper, who was leading the country in assists at the junior college level, committed to us the following week. And after striking out on a few more guys, we decided to recruit another transfer from Wyoming named Daylen Harrison. Daylen had the most supportive parents in our program and came from a great family. He was an only child, which caused him to be timid at times, but he helped us make a great impact. Dashonte, Glenn, and Daylen became known as our "Big Three."

The important high school recruit we felt we needed to change the program and make a splash was the one and only, Raven Lee. I met Ray right around the same time that Glenn Bryant came to visit. He was a junior in high school, and the most talented guard in the state of Michigan. Initially, I thought there was no chance we'd be able to get him in an Eagle uniform. But we decided to take a chance and keep recruiting him, regardless what the odds were. Coming out of high school, Ray had several high-major schools interested in him. But because we did such a good job recruiting him, we were always in the back of his mind as an option.

This is where the saying, "be careful what you wish for," was applicable. Sure enough, we landed Ray Lee, and I had no idea what I was in for coaching Ray for the next 5 years. Ray attended five different high schools in four years, and because of his talent, I ignored many red flags. Younger coaches tend to think we can tackle the world and mold anyone. The older me, now knows better. Experience is always the best teacher. Can you imagine coaching a student-athlete for 5 years that had as many stops in 4 years in high school?

As a first year head coach, I knew there was a lot more to learn, but I also knew I worked long and hard to prepare myself for this moment. Even though recruiting was my forte, I was a student of the game, and loved watching film. When I was an assistant at Kent State, I realized that I would always have to prove that I was just as knowledgeable about Xs and Os as the other coaches, so I was always prepared. The summer after I got the job at EMU, I experienced mixed reactions from other coaches when I walked into the gym to recruit. While most of my colleagues seemed happy that I got the opportunity, there were a few who threw a little shade.

"Hey, Murph, recruiting is important, but now you have to coach them, too," current Ohio State assistant coach Ryan Pedon said. "The MAC has really good coaching, so it won't be the talent that wins the game."

I couldn't believe he actually had the balls to say that to me, as if I were just a recruiter who could not coach! But I remained calm and cool, smiled and said "we shall see" while walking the other way.

As soon as my family was settled in Canton, Michigan, my time revolved around laying the foundation of a successful program. My first season, we were picked to finish twelfth out of twelve teams in our conference in every pre-season poll, which to me was unacceptable and would no longer be the expectation. We didn't have a team full of great talent, but I knew once my staff understood what we needed and our players bought into our new system, we would have a chance to be competitive and win some games.

There was a lack of confidence in the gym as we kicked off our first week of practice. Our players were accustomed to defeat, and my goal was to get these guys to believe that if we defended at a high level, we could stay in games and steal some victories. We were off to a great start as we opened the season, winning our first four games. The season dipped in the middle, but we finished strong in the end.

Playing Michigan State at home was one of the most exciting games for me in my first season as a head coach. Getting a chance to coach against the best program in the state and a long-time mentor, Tom Izzo, was a pretty cool feeling. We competed well in the first half as they struggled against our zone. But then their talent began to take over, and they pulled away in the second half with an easy victory. Draymond Green was the leader of that Spartan team. I remember yelling and screaming at my team at halftime, but now looking back, we had no chance of winning that game. At the time, I refused to believe we couldn't win.

Returning to Syracuse for a game against Coach Boeheim and the Orange was THE highlight of our non-conference schedule. Driving up to the Carrier Dome as a visitor felt so weird. Once we arrived, I was greeted like a celebrity on the red carpet. I could feel the adrenaline rushing through my veins when I walked into the Dome for a pre-game practice. All of the memories and experiences I had in that building came flooding back. When my players entered the Dome for the first time, they did so in complete awe. They had never played in an arena like this one. Practice went well, I fulfilled all the media requests, and before you knew it, it was GAME TIME!

"And now, a former Orange assistant coach, and now THE Head Men's Basketball Coach of Eastern Michigan University Coach, Rob Murphy!"

The Carrier Dome staff and all of the Orange fans cheered loudly when I walked on to the court. What a feeling! I looked up to a sea of orange cheering, and yet again, I couldn't help but tear up. It was an unexplainable feeling. Coaching back in the Dome against my mentor who played such a huge role in my growth, and being supported by the entire Syracuse community was… incredible. I tried to contain my emotions when KJ, C.J., Baye, Trice, Scoop, and the entire Cuse team came rushing over to greet me before tip-off.

We played extremely well in the first half, and went into the locker room down four points. Coach Boeheim played man-to-man defense in the first half, which allowed us to control the game on both ends of the floor. But five minutes into the second half came the Orange explosion! They went on a 14-0 run, and the lead grew to eighteen points. The game was pretty much over.

It's interesting to watch how a group of people or a person will respond in a moment when it's clear they aren't going to succeed. My team had no chance of beating the Cuse that night, but the game became a great indicator of who my best players would be. I spent the remainder of the game evaluating who was still playing hard, and who had already given into the loss. The players that were still playing hard knowing we would lose, understood consistency and commitment. Whether you're winning or losing, to be successful you have to give your all, all of the time. The most successful athletes in the world exemplify this.

It's safe to say that the game against Syracuse that night was an experience my players and I would never forget. Playing against the Orange was a great learning tool for my entire program. The exact same strategy I had been trying to implement all season was on full display. That game would help us get better moving forward.

As the MAC season approached, we were playing very well. The first half of the season we were in second place, and were shocking the world of basketball. A game winning 3-point shot by Antonio Green at Ball State made us believe we could beat anyone. Ball State was picked to win the West

Division, but we had other plans. We had another big win at home versus Western Michigan the following week, and everyone was calling us "butter" because we were "on a roll." The biggest game of the year was our second to last game against Western Michigan on the road. The MAC West title was at stake and a top four finish. The game went back and forth, and once it came down to the final play, we called a timeout with thirteen seconds to go. Could we really be in position to win a MAC West Title in my first season?

Darrell Lampley, our senior captain, executed the play to perfection with a scoop shot layup to take the lead by one point with two seconds left! Western threw up a full court prayer, wide left! We did it! For the first time in school history, Eastern Michigan won the MAC West Title. After the victory, we had a huge celebration in Western's locker room. Our AD, Dr. Gragg, came in to celebrate with us as well. I was so excited that the seniors would be able to hang a banner, and get fitted for a championship ring. Although there was more season left to go, we acted as if this was the end, which affected the following games, and caused us to have an early exit out of the MAC tournament.

That year, I was honored to be named the MAC and NABC District 14 coach of the year.

Chapter Twelve

FLY LIKE
AN EAGLE

After my first season at EMU concluded, it was time for professional development. My first development trip was to Oklahoma City to see watch the first round of the NBA playoffs where the Thunder were hosting the Dallas Mavericks. I was able to attend shoot-around on game day and speak briefly with head coach, Scott Brooks, about their game play to beat Dirk and the Mavs. Weave left Syracuse to work for the Utah Jazz, then ended up with the Thunder, and remains the Vice President of Basketball Operations. When I arrived in OKC, I learned through Weave that Rob Hennigan, who was on the Thunder staff, was a finalist for the Orlando Magic General Manager position. I knew Rob when he started out as an intern with the San Antonio Spurs years prior. Our relationship developed through his consistent calls to get background checks on players of interest for San Antonio. Throughout the years, Rob and I always maintained a good rapport. During halftime, I ended up running into Rob in the staff suite, and minutes later he was pulling me to the side for a private conversation.

"Murph, would you have any interest working at the NBA level?" he asked.

"Sure, I've always wanted to work at this level," I said.

"What side would you be interested in?" he inquired.

I didn't expect that question so I stammered, "Uhhhhh, probably the front office."

"Let's talk in the next few weeks."

"Sounds good, looking forward to it."

Talk about being in the RIGHT PLACE at the RIGHT TIME. If Rob landed the job, there would be a great chance I would have an opportunity to work for the Orlando Magic. The Thunder ended up winning that game against Dallas, and went on to win the series.

The next day, Weave called and mentioned he talked to Rob. Rob reiterated to Weave that if he landed the job, and I was ready to make the jump, there would be a spot for me working for the Orlando Magic. The last time Weave and I had a conversation similar to this was when I was invited to interview for the Syracuse position. As soon as I got off the phone with him, I started doing my research so that if the opportunity presented itself, I'd be prepared. Working in the NBA had always been a goal of mine, but a few things needed to be considered. Was I REALLY ready to leave my position as a head coach after making such a great impact at EMU in just one year?

As the weeks passed, I continued to do my homework. I wanted to be able to say YES without hesitation when I was offered the job. I remember talking to long time mentor, Scott Perry, who was newly hired in Orlando after leaving the Pistons, and asking what he thought about the move.

"Now, Murph, I'm gonna play devil's advocate with you. Understand something. You are a Division I head coach, meaning you are your own boss for the most part. Coming here, you're gonna relinquish that power and be working on someone else's watch. Are you sure you want to give that power up, and take a pay cut in the process? You don't need to answer that now, but that's something you need to think about. At this level, we meet, travel, meet again, and you make the call on none of it," explained Scott.

A couple of months later, Rob Hennigan was ready to make the offer, and before he did, Scott called one last time.

"Okay now, when Rob calls you, ain't no turning back," Scott said.

But before Rob could even call me, someone leaked the news, and the story broke around the country that I had already joined the Orlando Magic. My phone blew up with call after call and texts, and I hadn't even accepted a job or signed a contract yet! That's when my boss, Dr. Gragg, called me into his office.

"Rob, you can't leave to be an NBA scout. The timing is bad, and you've only been here one season. You were Coach of the Year, won the MAC West division title, and you're at home! Come on man, what are you thinking?" he asked.

"Derrick, I've been waiting on this opportunity a long time, it's my lifelong dream to work in the NBA," and before I could finish explaining my point of view, Dr. Gragg quickly cut me off.

"Rob, you cannot do this man. You're gonna kill your career, and I stuck my neck on the line to hire you here. Do you realize how hard that was? This will also hurt me as well. Go home and sleep on it; at least do that for me," he implored.

When the news broke about the Orlando Magic before the process was properly handled, it caused an uproar with my superiors at Eastern Michigan because they were completely caught off guard. Rob sent over the offer sheet to Nikki Borges, who was working as my agent during this process. Nikki did an amazing job representing me. She's one of the best communicators, and a shrewd contract negotiator. I signed the offer sheet a few days later, and was ready to take on what I believed to be my lifelong dream of working in the NBA. Right after I signed the offer sheet, Dr. Gragg reached out and offered me a salary increase to stay at EMU. But this decision had nothing to do with money. This was an opportunity to make a dream reality, and it was right at my fingertips. In one last attempt to convince me to stay, he set up a meeting with President Martin.

An hour later, we walked into the president's office. She was sitting with her arms crossed and ready to battle.

"Coach, I understand you wanna leave, but do you understand that we gave you an opportunity to work at EMU as our Head Men's Basketball Coach? No one wanted you here, but we went out on a limb and hired you. You're doing a good job, so tell me, what's it gonna take for you to stay at EMU?" President Martin inquired.

Dr. Gragg sat quietly listening the entire time.

"I'm sorry, but this is a great opportunity for me, and I don't believe there's anything that can be done to be honest," I replied.

"Are you telling me we gave you this opportunity, and you're gonna walk out on us like this? Well, if you leave, we're gonna release your entire staff. None of them can stay here, so that's something you need to think about. The timing is bad, and we don't deserve this," she stated.

Shocked by her ultimatum, I posed a question. "If Harvard called and offered you the position to be their president, would you turn it down?" She couldn't answer and just gave me a blank stare because the answer was obvious, she would take the opportunity. I told them I'd think about it, and politely excused myself from the meeting.

Once we left, Dr. Gragg and I rode silently back to the Convocation Center.

"Trust me Rob, you gotta think about this further. Call me tonight, and if this means anything, stay at Eastern for me," he said upon exiting the car.

When I got back home, TeNesha and I debated the pros and cons of each option. She was always against the idea of me leaving college basketball for an NBA position. The thought of me working in the NBA made her mind ponder profusely about hypothetical thoughts and situations that were inconsequential.

"How can you leave your staff members without jobs? It's late August, and there's no way they're gonna find work. It's just not fair, Rob," she pointed out.

I had to face the reality that this decision was much bigger than me. Based on what President Martin said, if I quit, then my entire staff would be unemployed. My decision would potentially affect the lives of at least five other people. I sat up all night contemplating before making my decision. The next day, I flew to Orlando to meet with Rob face to face to turn down the offer. It was tough, but it felt like the right thing to do. Rob agreed with EMU, and understood the timing wasn't the best. He also noted it might be a good idea for him to wait on making this hire for Orlando as well, at least until after the year passed. He thought that maybe I could revisit joining the Magic.

When I got back to EMU, I was relived to share the news with Dr. Gragg and my players. When I approached the locker room, I could feel the disappointment in the air. My team was confident that I was about to announce that I was moving on to the NBA.

"Gentlemen, there's been lots of speculation about me joining the Orlando Magic. The NBA has been a LONG time dream and goal of mine. Most of you, if given the opportunity, what would you do? Someone, tell me, what would you do?" I asked.

Glenn Bryant yelled out, "I would bounce, Coach, so we know you are bouncing!"

I chuckled at Glenn's response, and then began to explain the bigger picture. And when I told them I was turning down the opportunity to remain the Head Coach at EMU, the room erupted in jubilation. Watching my players celebrate my return made me feel better. There's no way I would be able to live with myself, knowing that five people would be out of a job if I left last minute. President Martin's threat definitely worked, but our relationship would never be the same moving forward.

With the drama behind us, I was excited for my second season. We had quite a few new faces, and a lot of support around the program. All of my transfers, including the big three (Glenn, DaShonte, and Daylen) were now eligible to play, and the team was prepared for a breakout season.

Shortly after the "Big Three" were committed the previous year, I received a call from Coach Tony Woods, Henry Ford Community College, who told me James Still had an interest in leaving the University of Detroit. James was a very nice kid from Detroit who I recruited during my time at Syracuse. James chose to attend Providence University out of high school, but was suspended from school for an assault. I learned that he had pending legal charges against him, and U of D did not want to honor the scholarship they promised to James because the assault charges still hadn't been dropped in Rhode Island. Even after I did my research, I believed in James, and felt I could continue to help him mature as a young man, while he helped rebuild the EMU basketball program.

James stood 6'10", could rebound, finish, and shoot from the outside. The talent was there, but it would be a challenge to get EMU to believe James was a good kid, and that his current assault charges would be dropped. I communicated the information to my athletic director, and he immediately told me NO!

"This is your first head coaching job, Rob, and as a new head coach you cannot take this chance early in your career. Do you believe James will make that much difference? It seems like you have some good players in place already," Derrick said.

My belief in James pushed me to explain to Derrick why I thought he was worth the risk. Reluctantly, Derrick took the next step and asked for the support of President Martin and Regent Stapleton. Both landed on a HARD NO!

Again, I shared my reasoning about why James was the right choice, and I brought up the fact that they were judging a kid based off one mistake and the person who was the defendant dropped the charges against James. Around the same time, I was also fighting to get Jordan Dumars (son of former Pistons' great, Joe Dumars) into school. Jordan was a walk-on at Michigan who wanted out, and I felt he was good enough to help our team. But President Martin did not want to admit him into school either, because of disturbing rumor she heard about him from her colleagues involving an altercation with another student on campus at Michigan. So, here I was, trying to convince her that we needed both James and Jordan.

A few days later, the President presented an offer to my AD, Derrick. If I let the Dumars situation go, she would sign off on James Still coming to Eastern. Coincidentally, earlier that morning, Joe called to tell me that Jordan was no longer interested in coming to EMU because they didn't need him attending a university where he wasn't wanted. I apologized to Joe, and he understood that I did everything I could.

After James graduated from Henry Ford Community College the following season, he was ready to attend EMU. James explained that he had grown since the incident at Providence. He completed a year at Providence University with a 2.6 GPA, the following year with a 2.8 GPA at the University of Detroit and then completed a year at Henry Ford finishing with a 3.3 GPA and graduated with his associate degree. The only hurdle left was the lingering charge that his attorney informed me would be eventually dropped.

Two long years went by, and James was still living with the uncertainty of what would happen. James was doing great academically. But after the second game of the season, Derrick decided to pull James off the floor and suspend him until the charges were completely dropped. It was very tough on James, and unfair because he worked very hard both academically and athletically to return to playing Division I basketball. On top of that, his next court date wasn't until Jan 22, 2013, which was seventy days and seventeen games away. Since James wasn't allowed to do any basketball related activities, he focused on keeping his grades up.

Finally, his court day was approaching. I called James into my office on Saturday to let him know I would be flying to Rhode Island to attend court with him on Tuesday.

"Coach, don't we play Western on Wednesday?" he asked.

"Yes, but I'll let my assistants handle the preparation for that game. Supporting you is more important to me," I stated.

James and I took the same flight to Providence on Monday evening. We ate dinner after checking into Marriott Hotel in downtown Rhode Island. I continued to be optimistic with James, hoping all the charges would be dropped the next morning, and we'd be on our flight back to Michigan.

The sound of the alarm woke me early Tuesday morning. After breakfast, we headed to the courthouse to meet with James' attorney, John Verdecchia, to see if he had any inside information before James was called up to face Judge Vogel. What happened next was truly a travesty. At 9:45 a.m., James was called and after reading the charges, Judge Vogel sentenced James to fifteen years in jail. We eagerly waited for her to say that the sentence would be suspended, and that James would be awarded probation, but he would not be that fortunate. She decided to suspend eleven of the fifteen years, and James was immediately hand cuffed and taken into custody. His attorney asked the judge if I could speak to her on his behalf, but she didn't want to hear anything I had to say.

The sound in that court room blurred in the background, and everything went in slow motion as I sat there hopeless. I could hear my heartbeat pumping, and my breaths were deep and slow. There was nothing I could do. Nothing. I got one last look at him before they took him out, and signaled him to be strong by taking my fist and tapping it over my heart. It was hard for me to walk out of the court room that day and accept the reality.

Going back to the hotel to check out and pack up James' belongings was very difficult. I called his family to give them the information, and all I could hear was screaming and crying through the phone. They were stunned to hear that he would be in jail for four years, and so was I. That afternoon, I flew back to Detroit and drove to Kalamazoo, Michigan to meet my team at the hotel prior to the Western game. In tears, I shared this experience and told them how critical it is to make smart choices.

One bad decision can change your life forever. James ended up spending the next eighteen months in prison before getting released. I wrote him at least once a month and spoke to him when he called. I'm proud of the way he responded to his situation. Instead of blaming the world and not accepting responsibility for his actions, James completed his sentence without ever complaining. Once he got out of prison, he came back to Detroit where he tried to continue his career in basketball, but more importantly, he earned his bachelor's degree.

We were off to a solid start in season two, racking up an early season victory against a powerful Big Ten team, Purdue, giving us a huge confidence boost. I could see that we were competing on a level that could make us contenders for the MAC championship. Suddenly, we lost Ray Lee to a broken his foot, and this changed the complexion of the season. From this point on, our season was like riding a roller coaster, up-and-down and all around we rolled. We finished sixth in the league heading into the MAC tournament. In the first round of the tournament, we hosted Northern Illinois at home, and dominated them to advance out of the first round. From there we hit the road, and headed to Cleveland for the remainder of the tourney.

We knew facing Miami-OH would be tough, but with consistent scoring from Derrick Thompson and a great defensive performance by DaShonte, we were determined to move on. In the quarterfinal game we ran into a very talented and hungry Western Michigan team. Led by Shane Winnington, they refused to lose that night. Shane claimed his spot as the best big man in the league, as he ended our season and went on to become MAC champions. Regardless, it was evident that the EMU program was approaching the next level so I was eager and excited to keep building a champion.

Once the MAC tournament was over, Dr. Gragg was offered a job as the Athletic Director at the University of Tulsa. Needless to say, he took the job without blinking an eye! We still laugh about the fact that I gave up an opportunity to stay at Eastern for him, but he bolted the first chance he got! He left me right in the dust when his opportunity came around. Dr. Gragg was never treated fairly during his tenure as the AD of EMU, so it was totally understandable why he jumped at the Tulsa opportunity. He was expected to produce specific results with a small athletic budget and no authority to make decisions, which is very difficult. I can't thank Dr. Gragg enough for giving me the opportunity to become the Head Coach of EMU, and also for pushing me to stay. There was so much growth on the horizon for the program and my career.

Fellow coaches and staff members have always told me that it's important that the AD that hires you remains in their position throughout your coaching tenure. I had been a part of two amazing programs at Kent State and Syracuse with great support from both administrations, I had no idea what that truly meant until Derrick's replacement, Heather Lyke, arrived at Eastern Michigan.

Once Dr. Gragg officially moved on to Tulsa, Melody Werner became the interim AD, and she did a great job. Working for her during the completion of my second season was a seamless transition. As the interview process for a new AD was going on, all of the coaches at EMU were hopeful that President Martin would hire someone that was fair and supportive of all of us. The financial challenges within the department made it important to hire someone who understood the landscape of Eastern Michigan Athletics. But during the search process, it was obvious that President Martin had no intentions of getting my input. She formed a search committee, and I was not invited to join. After the Orlando Magic situation, she avoided having to deal with me at all costs. Fortunately, Jim Stapleton, who was on the Board of Regents at the time, demanded that all the head coaches have the opportunity to meet with the AD candidates for twenty minutes when they came for on-campus interviews.

After meeting with the four candidates, most believed Nathan Pine was clearly the best choice overall, and that Heather Lyke and Josh Whitman were very intriguing second options. Heather made me believe that she would fully support me and the men's basketball program, while fighting to get the resources necessary to win. So, I recommended her as one of my final choices for the position. (Ironically, only three head coaches, out of 16, were in support of Heather when the votes went in.) Once the smoke cleared, Heather became our new AD.

Going into my third season, we had a group of competitors Eastern Michigan had not seen for a long time. Winning sixteen games the previous year was a major step for the program, but this year, it was time to take it to the next level. Fortunately, we landed All-American JUCO Forward, Karrington Ward. He was our first high-major athlete who had an ability to shoot from the outside. Dashonte, Glenn, and Daylen Harrison were back for their senior years, and enigmatic Ray was entering his sophomore season, along with eligible transfer Mike Talley. In addition, we had guards, Darrell Combs, Jalen Ross, and J.R. Sims, giving us tons of talent and depth.

We started the season 6-0 before going to Lexington, Kentucky to take on the storied Kentucky Wildcats. The game was close for thirty-three minutes before a few bad calls helped them stretch their lead, and we could never get back within striking distance again. We went on to play the toughest non-conference schedule in the MAC that season. We faced Purdue, Duke, Syracuse, UMass, and a host of other really good mid-major opponents to get us prepared for the MAC conference. The season was full of highs and lows, but we hit a positive stride toward the end. Going into the MAC tournament, we were ready, but we were fatigued in the semifinal game against Toledo after playing four games in five nights! I was extremely proud of our team after winning twenty-two games, and earning a post-season victory in the College Basketball Invitational.

No matter what we did, it seemed Heather had no interest in supporting the basketball program. Entering my fourth season, I tried my best to build a relationship with my new boss, but our contentious relationship progressively got worse. Shortly after her arrival, she fired our football and baseball coaches, both of whom were black, and it seemed like I was going to be next.

One day, our compliance office received an anonymous phone call claiming I broke an NCAA rule, and Heather launched a fruitless investigation that lasted five months. Even after I was proven innocent multiple times, she kept digging with hopes my tenure at EMU would end. I was forced to spend $10,000 in legal fees, and was glad when I was finally vindicated. Although it could have been a distraction for me, I was determined not to let the false accusations affect my focus on my team and staff. We completed the non-conference slate at 11-2, the best record to start a season in the history of the men's basketball program. We upset Michigan inside Crisler Center, coached by future Hall of Famer, John Beilein, which was a great accomplishment! We were solid in MAC play and managed to finish the season with 21 victories. We reached the quarterfinals of the MAC tournament, and competed in the post-season College Basketball Invitational tournament

(CBI). Fortunately for me, 4 presidents, 4 athletic directors and 9 years later, I remain at the helm of Eastern Michigan Men's Basketball.

> Anyone coaching in college athletics should challenge themselves to think beyond their team when you have an opportunity to benefit student-athletes from different sports. I am very proud of the fact that we have won games and graduated men's basketball players at an unprecedented rate, but I am equally proud that I have been an integral part of the fundraising and improvement of the athletic department in significant ways. During my time at EMU, I have personally spearheaded the fundraising of over $400,000.00 that has benefited all student-athletes with projects like our nutrition station. Additionally, I have worked with donors to spearhead initiatives like floor seating and seat wrap to make the Convocation Center a more intimate environment for all teams that compete there. Making an impact on the entire athletic department is beneficial and gratifying.

For eight years, I watched my wife put many parts of her life and goals on hold to pour every ounce of energy she had into our children. I am thankful to have married the kind of woman who was willing to put our children first, especially in the position I'm in, which requires a lot of my time and travel for half of every year. I always knew there would eventually come a time when TeNesha would be ready to return to the workforce or give her journalism career a chance. I often motivated TeNesha to take the broadcasting route because I felt she'd be great on camera because of her smile, charisma and comedic personality. It wouldn't be enough for her to raise our children without attempting to reach her goals. As the kids grew older, the topic started to bubble up regarding her career ambitions. It was clear to TeNesha each year when the season came to a close, there would always be the potential for me to get a better job that could result in a move. We also wanted to settle on a place to raise our children that offered great academics, community and social support. So, I asked her, "In a perfect world, where would you like to live? If I went to the NBA or took a bigger head coaching position, where would you love to call our home base if I had to commute?" She knew she didn't want to be in Michigan, and definitely didn't want to move back to Kentucky at that time. I mentioned Washington, D.C. as an option because she had close friends there. And then I asked. "What about moving back to Syracuse?"

TeNesha is the daughter of a military man, and spent most of her childhood moving place to place. Living in Syracuse for six years was a place she resided in longer than any other during her life. Because of my job, TeNesha was able to be introduced to certain circles and finally able to build true friendships and a home when we lived there, different from anything she ever experienced. When I considered these factors, I understood why she had a craving to get back to Syracuse once it was mentioned and could be attainable. TeNesha further explained that Detroit was a top ten market, and there was no way she could get an anchoring or reporting job there. The notoriety we received from the Syracuse community could potentially help launch her career. There was also uncertainty working for an AD who was not supportive and wanted me fired. With that weighing consistently on my brain, I figured this move would help protect my family if things did not work out at EMU.

After a few more conversations, the idea was turning into a reality. We were set on moving back to Syracuse to pursue her dreams. With my blessings, we agreed to return to Syracuse with our two children to make it home for the next few years to jump-start her career. She would rely on the connections we made in Syracuse to ease into the TV market. She planned to take classes at Onondaga Community College to refresh her reporting skills, and then position herself to attain a career in television, reporting or even anchoring the news as she once envisioned.

It was a huge sacrifice for her and the kids to leave Michigan. This move would only payoff if her career blossomed. Selfishly, I couldn't stand the idea of not being able to see my family every day. But I reluctantly let them move back to Syracuse. It was her turn to attempt to have a career which she desired so deeply. Not long after the move everything started falling into place. A couple calls led to a few meetings, which led to lots of opportunity. Before we could blink, TeNesha was reporting, then anchoring and then the ultimate goal, becoming a co-host on Bridge Street. TeNesha has become a local celebrity in Syracuse and great television personality.

Meanwhile, my focus remained on basketball and recruiting. It came to my attention that a future legend was brewing in Ypsilanti, MI. I decided to reach out to Coach EJ Bates to get a feel for how good his son, Emoni could be in the future. After learning a family friend, Auntie Gwen was common kin folk, I invited EJ up to my office. During our first meeting there was lots of comfortability as we had lots of things in common. We discussed life, the business of basketball, goals, aspirations and of course Emoni. "EJ, how good is he? Is he really as good as the hype?" EJ chuckled and pulled out his phone to show me video. After watching three to four minutes of workout footage all I could say is WOW! "He just turned 12 and in the 6th grade?" I remember asking... I began to watch more videos and told EJ I wanted to see him work out. A few days later I watched Emoni and could not believe what I was witnessing. At the end of the workout I said to EJ "He could develop into the next Kevin Durant... Your son is very similar to KD when he was coming out of the 9th grade". I said that with conviction because I evaluated KD and recruited him to come to Syracuse when he was in high school. "With the skill set and ability, if he continues to grow and work this hard, he'll be a Top 3 pick in 2022". I believe Emoni Bates will have the biggest impact on Michigan high school basketball since the departure of Chris Webber and Jalen Rose in 1991. Emoni is a special talent who has the desire and passion to be great! This type of player comes around Michigan once every twenty years. Stay tuned!

The two seasons that followed were the worst of my coaching career! My family was no longer there every day which started to become a struggle for me. Anytime you're consistently away from your spouse, there's a chance you can grow apart. It's a natural occurrence that more focus is geared toward the children as opposed to the companionship, during the early stages of their lives already, and with distance the relationship can become strained and complicated. Our team had numerous setbacks over these two years and won less than twenty games each season. Not having support from administration was a continued challenge. During these times, I started to believe Murphy's Law was a real thing! Especially after we were blatantly cheated out of a basketball game at home vs Ball State, January 23, 2016. This was the first time it was confirmed we were cheated because of my skin color. Todd Williams, Rob Kruger, John Gaston purposely did everything they could to take the game away from us. It was so obvious and egregious, that two of the officials were suspended multiple games and were not allowed to work the MAC tournament that season. This has continued to be an ongoing challenge for all black coaches in our game today, especially when the opponents' head coach is white. It will continue to fall on deaf ears and when there's no consistent accountability it will continue to be a struggle. When this incident happened, all I could hear ringing in my brain was Ern "Champ" McCullough saying, "Bro, you gotta get out of Eastern…Go to the NBA. There's too many obstacles for you to overcome to be successful that's out of your control coaching here. You're better and deserve better than this." I was humbled in many areas of my life during this time, but I remain committed to Eastern. Losing caused me to evaluate where the program stood and the direction we were heading. Our recruiting efforts were deteriorating, and the loyalty of some of my staff was in question. It was time to make changes.

Heather actually suggested that I let go of some of my staff after year five, and I used her suggestion to warn my staff about the future. We were at the end of the sixth season with a disappointing record of 16-17, and the improvement wasn't there after extensive conversations of what we needed to do for improvement. Contemplating who to let go on my staff was another tough moment I had to face as a head coach, but there were too many indications for me to ignore.

"Chris (Creighton) just had to fire his best friend and it was very tough for him to do. This is a business, Rob. You gotta make the tough decisions. It's in your best interest that you make staff changes," said Heather, during a meeting in her office.

After continued evaluation of my program the next few days, I called Mike, Benny and Dro separately into my office to have the conversations about what I planned to do moving forward. These were the most difficult meetings I ever had in my professional career. It was really difficult, but I had to let Mike and Benny go.

As season six ended, I needed to make some changes to the roster as well. Negative locker room chemistry cost us many victories. The jealousy and constant competition between seniors Ray and Willie Mangum became our downfall from start to finish. We had a bunch of players who were selfish and competed harder against each other than they did against our actual opponents. As a coach, I had never witnessed anything like it ever before, and I knew moving forward it couldn't happen again. The only good news I received after the 2016-17 season was that Heather was being hired as the new Athletic Director at Pittsburgh.

The end of this season also marked the conclusion of Ray's tenure with the Eagles. His loyalty to me and our program is something I will never forget, and his departure was bittersweet. Though he is a character, in every sense of the word, and tested my patience numerous times, I know deep down he was a good kid who was growing and learning. From the time he stepped on campus, until the day he left, Ray's antics kept me in meetings with administrators and his parents regarding issues that mostly had nothing to do with basketball. Ray proved to be a handful as he always found a way to be late to class, practice, sometimes games, and community service events.

Whatever ways he could exercise the rebel within, he did but I never believed his actions were purposeful. Somehow, we survived five colorful years with Ray. I always joked with my staff that they deserved an award, a raise, and a six-month vacation for pulling off the feat no one else could. Ray left as one of the top five all-time leading scorer in the history of EMU's basketball program. He scored 46 points in 24 minutes as a junior vs Miami-OH and scored 50 points in a rivalry game vs Central Michigan during his senior campaign. Hands down, one of the best guards I ever coached at any level of basketball. Through all the ups and downs, I could not have been more proud of Ray's overall growth. I am hopeful all he learned during his time at Eastern Michigan spurs tremendous success for him throughout his life. If I had a chance to coach Ray all over again I'd sign him today!

Entering my seventh season, I felt good about the way I restructured my staff. Dro was promoted to associate head coach, Matt Cline returned to be an assistant coach, I added Jimmy Wooten as another assistant coach, and LaKita Gantz was ready to settle in for year two as our director of basketball operations. In addition, our new AD, Scott Weatherbee was already proving to be a tremendous asset to our athletic department and genuine supporter of all programs in the department.

During the off season everything seemed to be moving in a positive direction until TeNesha and I decided we were not going to continue as life partners. This was a devastating decision. As I reflect, deciding to move apart for career advancement was the beginning of end. In life, we are constantly experiencing new things that reshape our perspectives and who we are. When I got married and we had children, I had one goal. I wanted my children to have everything I didn't, including two parents in their life and a family that functioned as a whole. I aspired to create this because it was uncommon where I grew up. I spent my childhood watching only two kinds of relationships: toxic relationships that failed miserably or happy relationships that lasted. Naturally, I wanted the latter. I was so convinced that my success would not only be measured by my career, but by a happy marriage with one person that I lived happily ever after with.

However, as I was rising further in my career and TeNesha was cultivating her own, it became clear that the distance caused us to grow apart. When I reflect back, deciding to move for career advancement was the beginning of the end. The distance caused constant speculation which led to many disagreements. Because of this we felt it was best to part ways. It was a devasting decision for us both, but we agreed it was important to acknowledge that our season together had come to a close.

In today's society it's not breaking news that the divorce rate has hit an all-time high. If a room of teenagers were asked if their parents are still together, very few would be able to say yes and even fewer would say their parents are happy. We are living in a world where it is extremely common for a child to pack a bag to go to dads on the weekend, leave a sperate set of hair ties at moms, have stepparents, and double holiday celebrations. Parents have endless debates over money, infidelity, the tone used in a text message, and time with the children. Divorce quickly turns adults into children.

A part of me felt like I failed, and I know that many parents experience the exact same feeling after making the decision to end an unhappy marriage. What I found later was that there's no one way to achieve happiness. You don't have to get it right the first time. It's similar to the mindset I teach my players. Lose two games, still win the third. Fail the first time, get back up and try again. And it is no different with love. I learned that it's ok. It's ok to change. It's ok to grow. It's ok to get it wrong. Sometimes it just doesn't work. Sometimes you grow apart. Sometimes you meet someone else. Sometimes things happen. We are always evolving and that is ok.

TeNesha and I landed on one common goal: be phenomenal parents to RJ and Ryann, while remaining good friends. Living 450 miles away from them was already a struggle but nothing felt worse than knowing that I wouldn't be able to be there physically to comfort them throughout this process. In an effort to minimize the impact to the children, we agreed it was best to wait until the end of the school year to tell them. But that plan took an unexpected turn.

I was preparing for practice one day and RJ called …

"Hey dad, mom told us today that we're not going to be together as a family any longer". "What are you talking about RJ" I replied. "Mom said you guys were going to be friends, and we are all still family, but you guys are not going to be married anymore".

"What?!?! When did your mother tell you this and where is Ryann?" I said. "Ryann is in her room crying. Mom told us when we were riding in the car on our way to drop Ryann at gymnastics practice. Ryann started shouting and crying and told mom she did not want to go to practice, so we all just came back home" said RJ.

I could not believe this was happening. Holding the phone, I paused and stared at the gym ceiling confused, infuriated and sad all at the same time. I couldn't understand what triggered TeNesha to abruptly tell our children we were separating. We had an agreement to sit them down together and talk it out at the right time. She couldn't have thought on the way to gymnastics was the right time!

"RJ, where's your mom? Please put her on the phone" I demanded. "Hey Rob" says TeNesha. "TeNesha, why the hell would you tell the kids so abruptly? We agreed to tell them together at the end of the school year. I don't understand what happened to our plan" I responded. "I felt they needed to know instead of waiting any longer. Is there ever a perfect time? I don't think there is, so I just decided to tell them" TeNesha replied. "It may not be a perfect time but today without me being present was definitely not the right time! You could've waited until the next time I came to town, which would have been this weekend or next. This is BS TeNesha and you know it, let me talk back to RJ please." I apologized to RJ and promised him everything would be ok. I then briefly spoke with Ryann and told them both I'd call them right after team meetings. I hung up the phone and darted into practice and thought of nothing but my children the entire time until I was able to walk out the gym and call them back.

I'm sure there were several factors I was unaware of on TeNesha's end that sparked this moment to happen prematurely. Our relationship and ideas were no longer in alignment, which made it easier for other people's opinions to add pressure around the situation. Furthermore, in the small town of Syracuse with my notoriety as a former assistant coach and TeNesha's emerging spotlight as a news anchor, rumors began to swirl. As legitimacy continued to surface behind the rumors, the anguish and rush TeNesha was experiencing now made sense.

I knew both of my children were struggling but for Ryann in particular this was life altering. We made a huge mistake of not sitting down with them together and sharing the change more delicately. I was determined to do everything in my power to correct the process, so as to minimize the damage.

When I got to Syracuse that weekend, I started with reassurance. I reassured them that the love and bond we have as parents would never change. It was also important to help them understand that it's alright to have emotions about what's happening but more important to always share those emotions with mom and dad. Once they understood the separation had nothing to do with them and that the love, attention and affection for them would never change, they began to feel a little better. As time has passed, neither child has fully accepted the reality. Time has also revealed several disturbing things between TeNesha and I that we're continuing to work through so our kids will be affected as little as possible. I've allowed my focus to be our children which will always be at the forefront. Living apart to help TeNesha's career aspirations take off helped soothe our separation as well. Our children did not experience an abrupt "move out" of either parent because they were already accustomed to me commuting the past four years.

There is no question that a divorce is hard on everyone in the picture. If the children continue to feel loved by both parents and the parents work together to create a stable and calm environment, the children can emerge from a divorce in good shape. Parents should avoid talking badly about each other or placing blame, even in the midst of frustration. Children need both of their parents and it only causes an adverse effect to manipulate the child against the other parent. RJ and Ryann have done a great job remaining neutral and placing no judgement on either end. They also do a good job expressing themselves in a healthy way, and that's a credit to the open lines of communication we, as parents, have encouraged. I do my best to stay positive during all situations no matter what's said from the opposite side. This has definitely helped.

Season seven was set up for great success. This group brought an undeniable synergy. After losing seven players, many people doubted us. And even though we were picked to finish eighth overall and fourth in the West, I knew that we could absolutely contend for a MAC title! I witnessed our transfers compete daily against our starters and dominate them on some days. Paul Jackson and Elijah Minnie were particularly impressive; they already looked like All-MAC selections. We opened up the season winning six of our first eight games, including signature non-conference wins against Oakland at home, and a tough road victory at Long Beach State.

It appeared that we would roll through conference play with our momentum, but that was not the case. We started MAC play 2-6 including two home losses, causing some concern. From there, our results were erratic, and a loss to Western Michigan dropped us to eleventh place. I was trying everything I could to motivate the team, but nothing seemed to work. If I had any hair, I probably would've lost it all!

I received a visit from EMU Football Coach Creighton, who told me about the "bounce back" concept that he preaches to his team in situations like the one we were in. I listened closely, took his advice, and used the motivation technique with my team. After that, our guys totally bought into the bounce back concept, and we won eight of our next nine games, finishing third place overall in our league. It was the best record an EMU basketball team finished with in twenty-two years in conference play!

We entered the post-season as one of the hottest teams in the country. We flourished on offense, and our defense stifled our opponents. We lead the MAC conference in seven defensive categories and lead the country in combined blocks and steals. Tim Bond was named the Defensive Player of the Year. He led the conference in steals and became EMU's all-time steals leader. James Thompson IV was named to the All-MAC first team, and Elijah and Paul were respectively named to the second and third teams. A big quarterfinal win against Akron lead us to our third battle with Toledo in the semifinals. We ended up losing a heart breaker, which ended our NCAA tourney hopes, but we went on to compete in the CIT post-season tournament. With twenty-two wins overall, the Eagles were back!

Every spring, college coach's around the country have to coddle the unrealistic dreams of their players believing they are ready to play in the NBA. The dream is where it starts but the pressure from families, agents, AAU coaches and significant others cloud the brain of the student-athlete. Ninety percent of parents thinks their son is going to get drafted to play in the NBA and realistically there's less than a one percent chance that they'll ever play in the NBA. I was forced to entertain the unrealistic dreams of James Thompson (2nd time) and Elijah Minnie entering the NBA draft. During our exit meetings I shared information that I received from the NBA league office and seven general managers from NBA organizations. I was positive but brutally honest with James and Elijah with the information that was shared with me. Obviously, my information did not match up with the feedback given to the families from different agents. Without fail, they believed what their families and agents said over me, who was speaking to the decision makers during the long (two month) process. I knew what the end results would be after speaking with the decision makers and not the evaluators, which I explained during our meetings. My concern was how would they be affected after the woman of their dreams (NBA) turned them down. The pressure of improving your overall game is challenging, and when you add auditioning for the NBA, it brings more pressure than you can imagine. I had no idea this is where the Roller Coaster ride would begin for the following season!

Chapter Thirteen

A TAKABISHA SEASON

O nce the big three (James, Paul & Elijah) decided they would return we felt we had a chance to be a good basketball team. I flirted some with the NBA myself (opportunity with the New York Knicks) after the season but during the process I learned that I was supported more than ever by the entire EMU administration. I was awarded a contract extension by my administration for the first time during my tenure at EMU. It was made clear to me that I was being rewarded for the men's basketball's overall academic, athletic and community service success the past seven years. I immediately turned all my focus to competing for a MAC championship. Replacing Tim Bond was the first order of business which would be our toughest task. After a long spring recruiting process and a few commits we were ready for summer workouts!

My staff and I did a tremendous job focusing on the individual improvements of our roster with thoughts to enhance the overall skill level of our team. Every player was ready to work to position ourselves to have a great season. There are zero minutes available during the summer so frustrations of not starting or not playing never come into play which became a problem once the season was in full swing.

I had several concerns as official practice approached. I felt we signed a solid class but not a talented enough class that could replace the senior leadership we lost. The new additions had good skill level but lacked leadership qualities and the intangibles needed to make a huge impact. Our returning seniors, James Thompson IV, Paul Jackson and Elijah Minnie, had no desire to lead anyone other than themselves. After testing the "NBA waters" it damaged their perception on why they should come back to school. They were only worried about what they needed to do to enhance their NBA draft stock for the 2019 draft. After doing extensive homework, myself, along with several educated people, shared with them that the only way to improve draft stock was to win the MAC championship and participate in the NCAA tournament. Preaching winning didn't resonate as the most important goal, because families and agents sent a different message. The departure of our glue guys, Tim Bond and Jordan Nobles, both seniors who competed in our program four years, was noticeable. They were the leaders who galvanized everyone the previous season. I continue to believe being a leader is a talent and already within. Very seldom, can leadership be learned after already attending college. Recruiting leadership is very important to the success of any program.

After a month into practice we decided to scrimmage our alumni. It was two weeks before our first game. Shortly after the scrimmage, I whispered to our associate head coach, Kevin Mondro, "Dro I don't mean to be negative but this could be a long season" Dro replied "Guys were not here mentality today for whatever reason". "It's a bigger picture Dro, this will be a challenge all season, we have no leaders… these guys don't get it". With every practice thereafter it became more glaring, day by day, that "The Big Three" were all about themselves. We had no leaders in the locker room who could collar these guys to help give us the opportunity to reach our full potential over the next 150 days.

By the middle of the non-conference slate, I was disappointed that our fans would never get a chance to experience what was sold to them in the pre-season. Coaching my 23rd straight season, I had experienced enough teams to know and understand how this could potentially play out. My staff and me continued turning over every rock to avoid the inevitable. Contrary to popular belief, experience and senior does not equal leader.

After a disappointing MAC season, the only positive accomplishments the senior's received were for individual performance. James, Paul and Elijah all became 1000 point scorers. It's disappointing that's how this senior class will be remembered. Once the season was complete, the seniors were extremely hurt, but there was nothing that could be done to ever compete at the college level again. During our exit meetings they admitted the "We over Me" motto that I preach daily was the main ingredient missing from the team. James Thompson IV explained that each senior, including himself, felt the pressure of playing well to set themselves up for professional opportunities oppose to playing together as a team to win a championship. It was good hearing a valuable lesson was learned which should help their future success. It takes consistent sacrifice and togetherness (from every individual in the corporation) to have the best opportunity to compete for a championship.

What usually happens with failure and disappointment? Anger, hurt, sadness, sickness, frantic, doubt, delirious, worried, annoyed, ferocious, disgusted, livid and unhappy. Not Rob Murphy! With vivid reflection and honest evaluation comes truth and reality. The only thoughts I had was BOUNCING BACK! My staff and I met the following two days after our disappointing season. We worked on a master plan to put us in position to compete for a MAC title next season. We knew it would be a challenge to replace our experienced seniors, but with ten scholarships available we were excited to add many ingredients we knew were missing. Coach Wooten had been scouring the country all year and with keen evaluation from our entire staff we planned on filling our roster with a great 2019 class. Shortly after our Wednesday afternoon meeting, I quickly headed to the airport to fly to France. I felt Paris would be the perfect place help adjust my mindset before tackling the challenge ahead.

.

Overtime

BOUNCE BACK!

"Whatever you do and whatever situation you are in, you have to bounce back. We all must have the bounce back mentality. You can be this bean bag in my hand, you can be that egg cracked on the ground, or you can be this ball. If you throw all three, only one will bounce back. The key in anything you do is this (throws ball to the ground, it bounces back up) – you got to bounce back, just like this ball. Take me, age thirteen, I lost my mother. Boom! Big hit! Lots of heartache and struggle! What did I do? I bounced back! With all the adversity you will go through in your life, the key will always be how you bounce back."

Ultimately, we all hope to find our purpose in the time we spend here on this earth. God gave each of us a unique set of gifts to contribute to the world, and the key is discovering how you can use whatever talent God blessed you with to make a difference in the lives of others. I learned very early on what I was undeniably good at, and honed it to reach this level. What I didn't realize, until later, was precisely what my purpose is. I am not just a basketball coach. I am not just good at recruiting players and winning basketball games. I have been specifically placed in the lives of young men at one of their most pivotal points in life, to make an impact far beyond a basketball court.

Many of the young men I've encountered through my career would have never had the opportunity to go to college if they didn't get a scholarship to play basketball, let alone graduate and be prepared to lead successful lives off the court. My purpose is to help these young men, many of whom grew up with challenges like me, realize that they do not have to be products of their environment. That it is possible to resist the temptation of drugs, alcohol, and criminal activity, even if it's contaminating your neighborhood and everyone around you. And basketball is the avenue I've been granted to do that.

While basketball is a wonderful sport that has given me much joy and opportunities, the most important thing I have wanted my players to understand is that they need to graduate and get their degrees. Although just about every player has aspirations to play in the NBA or in Europe, the reality is only a very small percentage of players are lucky enough to collect a check once their college basketball career is over. After eight years leading the EMU Men's Basketball team, we have graduated 30 of 32 student athletes, and we have the highest GPA in the history of our basketball program, with our APR in excellent shape. Our program mantra, the Triple E's (Energy, Effort, Execution), has been beneficial helping my staff and student-athletes maintain consistent success, in all areas of our basketball program, over the past 8 years.

Despite my rough upbringing, I was fortunate to have people come into my life and guide me in the right direction. I will forever be grateful for everyone who encouraged me and made me feel that there was a possibility for me to defy the odds. With motivation from Shane McMullan, I've been able to refocus on the importance of fitness, nutrition and rest. Having this piece of self-maintenance become routine, has made an incredibly positive impact on my life. My vision is to do that for the next generation and help as many children as I can. With the help of Nikki Borges, on June 15, 2014,

I created The Rob Murphy Foundation. Nikki was my colleague at EMU, and she was instrumental in helping shape my vision for the Rob Murphy Foundation ("Every Child Deserves Opportunity"). The funding for the foundation was kicked off by some very generous donors, led by John Leigh. I'm also thankful for Eastern Michigan alumni, Dr. Robert Sims and Keith Stone (CSI) for their tremendous financial and emotional support of the not only the men's basketball program, but of the Foundation as well. The generosity of these men made a HUGE impact on our ability to serve the community in our first few years. Since the start of the foundation, we have been able to help more than 6,000 children and their families in the Detroit and Ypsilanti areas, starting with my very own Bagley Elementary School. I will continue to do as much as I can for as many people as I can.

Sometimes the plans you have for yourself aren't aligned with the plans God has laid out for you. When you finally understand what your purpose is in the grander scheme of life, your personal goals become less important and you become most fulfilled.

So, here I sit in a floor seat in an empty arena filled with green chairs, staring above at the white banners that line the perimeter of the arena. My eyes pause when I land on a banner with the West Title Championship. I take a deep inhale and let it out. I lean forward in my chair now, looking at the court floor. The lights are still up; faintly in the background, I hear reporters wrapping up their equipment. The janitors are going through the stands for any garbage the fans have left behind. In my hand is a small yellow and green laminated play card that lists twenty different plays. Twenty different plays designed to win a simple game. A simple game that will change so many young men's lives. I sit back in the chair again and cross my arms looking into the stands, and there she is… my mother… just sitting there looking right at me with a grin that says she's proud. I stand up, my heart drops. Stuck there, I don't take my eyes off her as she smiles back at me. She stands and slowly starts to clap her hands. Her clapping speeds up, and I try my best to swallow my emotion. I begin to cry…

How did I get here, you ask? I'm not exactly sure how to answer that question because I can't trace my success back to an exact decision or specific moment. There were various steps and experiences, each one leading to the next, that brought me to this point. But the key underlying threads have always been determination, consistency, hard work, a positive mindset, passion, circumstance, talent, commitment, and GOD.

A quick rhythm of small sneakers running across the court catches my attention. I quickly look away.

"Daaaaad, what are you doing? Why are you crying? You won (yanking on my arm)! Come on Daaaad, let's go!" says Ryann.

I look back up into the stands, and this time the seat is empty. I smile and stand there for one more moment. Then I throw Ryann over my shoulders, and the lights go down as we walk out the Eastern Michigan University Convocation Center.

Thank you for staying on this journey with me, reading a story I've never felt comfortable sharing. I hope that you can take something and relate it to your own life, challenges, ideas, goals, or beliefs, so that you too can use your circumstance to make an impact in the world, no matter how big or small. After all, that is why we're here!

SPECIAL THANKS

*Andrea Jean Murphy *Annie Mae Pierson *TeNesha Handley *Robert (RJ) Murphy II *Ryann Andrea Murphy *Sonny Pierson *Willie Murphy *James Payne *Ray Coleman *The Cottrell Family *The Washington Family *The Wright Family *The Bailes Family *Deon Griffin *Dr David Porter *Greg Cannon *Venius Jordan *Robert Lynch *Deanna Crowder *Marsha Keyes *RaRedding Murray *Oronde Taliaferro *Aaron Hayden *Antonio Gates *Maurice Ager *Andre Johnson *The Foster Family *Lance Williams *Doris Rodgers *Wallace Whitfield *Tim Ferguson *Scott Perry *Jim Christian *The Handley Family *Jim Boeheim *Troy Weaver *Donte Greene *Giovanna McCarthy *Mike Rubenstein *Derrick Gragg *Jim Stapleton *Sue Martin *Roy Wilbanks *Nikki Borges *Keja Jones *Eastern Michigan University Men's Basketball Staffs and Student-Athletes, Murphy Era *Syracuse & Kent State University Men's Basketball Staffs & Student-Athletes, Murphy Era *Crockett & Central High School Boy's Basketball Student-Athletes, Murphy Era *Chris Grier Luchey *Will Smith *LaBaron German *Central State University *Mumford High School *Beaubien Middle School *Bagley Elementary *Cobras & Cougars Youth Football Programs *Tindal & Johnson Recreation Centers

Rob Murphy, Bagley Elementary, 5th Grade

Andrea Jean Murphy, Mother

Rob Murphy, Central State University, Freshman Year

Andrea Jean Murphy

Andrea "Suddie" Murphy

(Always the Life of the Party)

Torin Cottrell & Rob Murphy, 6 years old

Rob Murphy

Mumford Mustangs vs Northern Jayhawks

Rob Murphy

Mumford High School

10th Grade

Rob Murphy

Central State University

Junior Year

St Thomas, Virgin Islands

Eyes on the Prize

Central State University

Graduation Day

Crockett Basketball

"The Big Three"

Adams, Knight & Ager

Aunt Gloria, 70th Birthday Party

James "Woo" Payne

Brother

Aaron Hayden, Best Friend

Antonio Gates

Las Vegas

Tenesha, RJ & Ryann

EMU Basketball Game

NBA Playoffs

My Happy Place

The Eastern Michigan Eagle

Come Soar with the Eagles

Kareem Hailey

Childhood Friend

Lance Williams

Big Three Championship

Las Vegas

Jay Z Concert - Detroit

My Happier Place

Anthony Wilkins

Floyd vs Berto

Las Vegas

RJ Murphy

Raisin in the Sun

(acting debut)

RJ & I

(chilling during play rehearsal)

Robert Murphy II & Ryann Murphy

GOD's Greatest Gifts

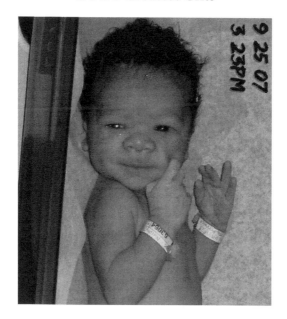

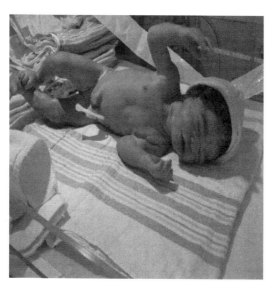

The Murphy Family for the birth of Ryann Murphy

EMU Press Conference - April 21st, 2011

greatest basketball accomplishment thus far

God Mother, Marsha Keyes

with RJ & Ryann

Nothing more exciting, than a rally

in the Carrier Dome!!!

Coach RJ Murphy

EMU Basketball - Summer Tour

Atlantis, Bahamas

Ray Lee

Dynamic Scorer

Tim Bond

EMU Senior Day

Madison Square Garden

Big East Tournament Champions

James Thompson IV

(picture day shenanigans)

.

One on One

vs Tim Bond

(picture day)

Ryann Murphy

Gold Medal Gymnast

RJ's

5th Birthday

The Murphy's

EMU Press Conference - April 21st, 2011

Dr Robert Sims

First African American basketball player

to compete at Eastern Michigan University

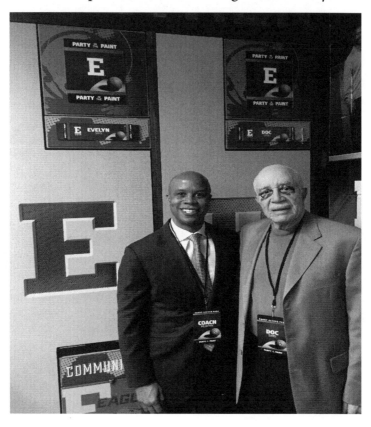

George "Ice Man" Gervin

Visiting with EMU basketball

NBA & EMU Basketball Hall of Fame

My Favorite Senior Class

Ypsi Awards

EMU Basketball Squad

Rob Murphy Foundation

Bagley Elementary School

Nikki Borges

Rob Murphy Foundation Chair

Rob Murphy Foundation

Boys & Girls Club

EMU Hoops & Dance Team

Shut It Down

Our Team Anthem in 2009

The Best Coach/Rapper Alive

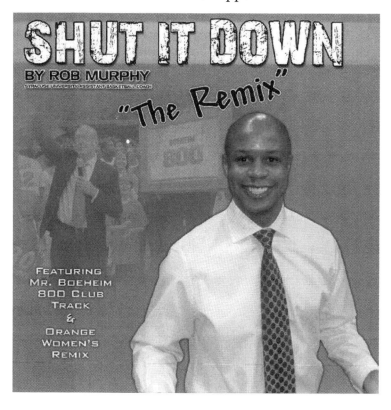

Jim Boeheim

I'm forever thankful

for the life changing opportunity

Jim Boeheim & Mike Hopkins

The Zone Trust

A few favorite Orangemen

Maurice Ager – We Trusted the Process

EMU Basketball Staff's

EMU Basketball

Atlantis, Bahamas

My Favorite Day of the Year

Father's Day
2014

Keith Stone

EMU Alum

CSI Enterprises

Supporting the Rob Murphy Foundation

Bagley Elementary

Donte Greene & Kris Joseph

My Favorite Oranges

Game Day Victories

Bring Huge Smiles

EMU Alums are the BEST!!!

Victoria Sun

BEST DOBO of ALL TIME!!!

(director of basketball operations)

Eastern Michigan 45

University of Michigan 42

Impossible without great Players & Staffs

· GRATITUDE

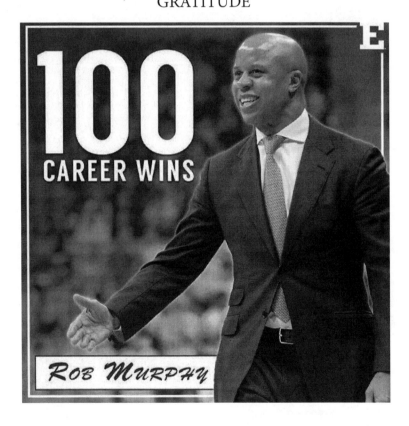

Live the Phrase

SKY'S THE LIMIT

Swimming with Dolphins

Atlantis, Bahamas

Lacrosse Tournament

Ryann's a Versatile Athlete

Rob Murphy Foundation

Reading Challenge

"Every Child Deserves Opportunity"

Aaron "Tron" Williams

College Teammate

The Boeheim's

RJ & Ryann

RaRedding Murray

Best Friend

President Jim Smith & wife Connie

Receiving the game ball after their first EMU basketball game

Coach Murphy and Antonio Gates

Kent State vs Boston College

Gund Arena – 2002

DEFENSE FIRST

2014 - #1

DEFENSIVE TEAM

in the COUNTRY

Dave Bing

Former Mayor of Detroit

NBA & Syracuse - Hall of Famer

RJ & Ryann

Michael Jackson ONE

Red Carpet – Las Vegas

Dr. Derrick Gragg

2012 - MAC West Champs

Ring Ceremony

Dante Darling Sr.

Central High School

EMU Alum

Detroit Crockett – 2001

District, Regional & State Champions

Ascending moment that gave confirmation

Coach of the Year - 2001

Uncle Skeeter & Ryann

Christmas - 2010

The pamphlet and interview that helped PREPARE

me to become the Head Coach at

Eastern Michigan University

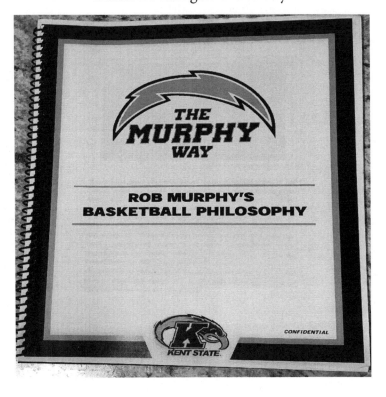

Leave a Legacy

Eastern Michigan University

Student-Athlete Performance Center

We Are Forever Eagles

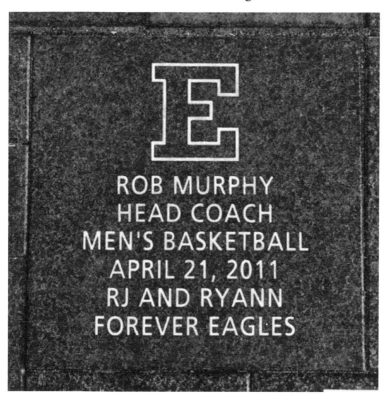

Heart Breaking Loss

vs River Rouge HS

My last game coached at Crockett Technical High School

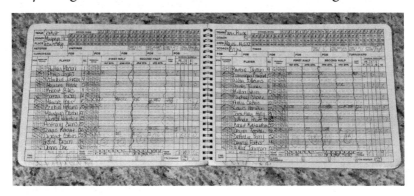

Ryann's 9th Birthday

Las Vegas, Nevada

DUO

Jimmy Tyman, Chris Grier Luchey,
Daryl Greer, Will Smith, Antonio Gates

The ALMIGHTY continues to BLESS ME with Great Life Experiences!!!

The Wave of the FUTURE!!!

OPEN GATES